T0360435

.

ROUTLEDGE LIBRARY EDITIONS:
FOOD SUPPLY AND POLICY

Volume 6

HUNGER AND FOOD ASSISTANCE POLICY IN THE UNITED STATES

HUNGER AND FOOD ASSISTANCE POLICY IN THE UNITED STATES

REGINA GALER-UNTI

Routledge
Taylor & Francis Group

LONDON AND NEW YORK

First published in 1995 by Garland

This edition first published in 2020
by Routledge
4 Park Square, Milton Park, Abingdon, Oxon OX14 4RN
605 Third Avenue, New York, NY 10017

Routledge is an imprint of the Taylor & Francis Group, an informa business

British Library Cataloguing in Publication Data
A catalogue record for this book is available from the British Library

ISBN: 978-0-367-26640-0 (Set)
ISBN: 978-0-429-29433-4 (Set) (ebk)
ISBN: 978-0-367-27576-1 (Volume 6) (hbk)
ISBN: 978-0-429-29675-8 (Volume 6) (ebk)

Publisher's Note
The publisher has gone to great lengths to ensure the quality of this reprint but points out that some imperfections in the original copies may be apparent.

Disclaimer
The publisher has made every effort to trace copyright holders and would welcome correspondence from those they have been unable to trace.

HUNGER AND FOOD ASSISTANCE POLICY IN THE UNITED STATES

REGINA GALER-UNTI

GARLAND PUBLISHING, Inc.
New York & London / 1995

Library of Congress Cataloging-in-Publication Data

Galer-Unti, Regina, 1956–
    Hunger and food assistance policy in the United States /
Regina Galer-Unti.
        p.   cm. — (Children of poverty)
    Includes bibliographical references and index.
    ISBN 0-8153-2175-9 (acid-free paper)
    1. Food relief—United States—History. 2. Poor—United
States—History. 3. United States—Social Policy. 4. Public wel-
fare—United States—History. 5. Hunger. 6. Malnutrition—
United States. I. Title. II. Series.
HV696.F6G25 1995   95-25281
363.8'83'0973—dc20

Printed on acid-free, 250-year-life paper
Manufactured in the United States of America

Dedication

To my parents, Nancy and Eugene Unti.

Contents

Tables

Table

Preface

The idea for this study emerged in the 1980s when I was a graduate student in Health Policy at the University of Illinois at Urbana-Champaign. At that time, the evening news bulletins were rife with reports of the existence of a widespread hunger problem in the population of the United States. Pictures of long lines of people queued up at food banks and soup kitchens seemed inconsistent with the view of America as the "land of plenty." Additionally, there was great disagreement about the incidence and prevalence of hunger in the United States. While some groups claimed that millions were hungry, others declared that there were no hungry people in America.

During this time period a documentary entitled, "CBS Reports: Hunger in America," was shown in one of my health classes. The film, made in 1968, showed hunger in Appalachia and the deep South. I wondered why, after so many years, this problem of hunger had emerged again as an issue. I wondered also if the data would show a rise in hunger during the 1980s.

So, I began to search for the data about hunger that had been collected since this documentary had been produced. I was surprised to find that, although many food assistance programs had been inaugurated during the 1960s and 1970s, very little data had been collected about hunger in the United States. The success or failure of health policy is tempered by the existence and access to accurate data by policy makers. In the absence of a government system for the measurement and collection of such data, it fell upon the churches, states, and private agencies to collect information about the swelling ranks of individuals seeking emergency food assistance.

In light of this information, I decided it would be interesting to investigate two things. First, it would be useful to look at the results of the studies that had been collected in the U.S. during this time frame (i.e.,

1980s). Second, it would be useful to examine the history and development of hunger and food assistance policy in the U.S. These two components would provide, I felt, an excellent foundation for the study of this type of health policy. Information from this analysis would be used to make recommendations for future data collection efforts, food assistance policy formulation, and nutrition policy decisions in the U.S.

I collected hunger studies that had been conducted in the U.S. during the decade of the 1980s and began to assess their design, and quantitative and qualitative information. I spent a considerable amount of time finding these surveys. Information about these studies resided in a variety of different databases. Many of the studies were difficult to find because they were unpublished. Many of the studies were unusable because of sloppy scientific technique. After locating all studies, the systematic methodology of meta-analysis was employed in order to provide a framework for this investigation. Meta-analysis proved to be a worthy guide for this study. Although I did my bookkeeping, if you will, by hand, I understand that there are computer programs that aid in keeping track of the qualitative portions of a meta-analytic investigation.

A number of individuals aided in the completion of this book. For their help, advice, and friendship I am truly grateful.

I thank the members of my dissertation committee (Dr. Laurna Rubinson, Dr. R. Warwick Armstrong, Dr. Dale Rublee, and Dr. M. Margaret Weigel) for the time and energy that they expended in aiding me with my work. A special thanks to Dale Rublee. I am grateful to him for his initial help in formulating the idea for the project and his patience and willingness to see it through to the end.

Lynn Parker of the Food Research and Action Center in Washington, D.C. was kind enough to allow me to use her files. The use of these files was of critical importance to this study and I thank her for her indulgence.

I would also like to thank Dr. Marlene Tappe of Purdue University. She provided both professional help and friendly advice which aided tremendously in the completion of this study.

Finally, I would like to acknowledge the support that my family has given me. Thanks to Tom Galer-Unti for his assistance with the formatting of this manuscript. I would particularly like to recognize my daughter, Caitlin Elizabeth Galer-Unti for her patience when I had to work, and her helpfulness in photocopying and locating journal articles.

Hunger and Food Assistance Policy in the United States

I

Introduction

In the early 1980s reports of widespread hunger among members of the U.S. population began to appear in the media. Throughout the decade this phenomenon of "hunger in the land of plenty" was continually reported and debated. Hundreds of national, state, and local studies were undertaken by churches, private agencies, and government agencies in an effort to document the existence and extent of hunger in the U.S. The President's Task Force on Food Assistance studied the problem in 1984, but found no evidence of widespread hunger. In 1985 the Harvard-based Physician Task Force on Hunger in America [Physician Task Force] estimated that 20 million Americans were experiencing hunger while 40 million were at risk of hunger. This lack of agreement with regard to the incidence and prevalence of the problem was argued throughout the 1980s (Brown and Allen 1988). The confusion over the issue is exemplified by statements such as the one in 1988 by then Surgeon General C. Everitt Koop. In his opening letter to *The Surgeon General's Report on Nutrition and Health*, Koop stated:

> "The apparently sizeable numbers of people resorting to the use of soup kitchens and related food facilities, as well as the possible role of poor diet as a contributor to the higher infant mortality rates associated with inadequate income, suggest the need for better monitoring of the nature and extent of the problem and for sustained efforts to correct the underlying causes of diminished health due to inadequate or inappropriate

diets." (United States Department of Health and Human
Services [USDHHS], 1988, p. iv)

The *Surgeon General's Report on Nutrition and Health was*
developed as an authoritative source of information about the relationship
between diet and disease and was designed to be used as the basis for U.S.
nutrition policy decisions (McGinnis and Nestle 1989). Yet hunger, and its
related physiologic and behavioral problems, was not addressed in the
report.

Despite the lack of agreement about the nature and extent of the
hunger problem, there is agreement in the scientific community that
hunger can have particularly detrimental health consequences for the
individual. Malnutrition is a serious health threat and this is especially true
for vulnerable population segments such as pregnant and lactating women,
infants and children, and the elderly (Guthrie 1979; Robinson et al. 1986).
Authors of some studies suggested that there had been an increase in
indicators of health problems associated with inadequate nutrition during
the decade of the 1980s (Physician Task Force 1985; USDHHS 1988).
Brown and Allen (1988) reported an association between poor diet and
elevated infant mortality rates. Polhamus, Peterson, and Miller (1989)
documented poor diet in a low income group of Boston children and a
relationship with failure-to-thrive syndrome.

This was not the first time that hunger appeared as a prominent
national issue. Hunger and malnutrition became the topics of national
security during World War II when a noticeably large number of draftees
were rejected because of nutrition-related health disorders (Food Research
and Action Center [FRAC] 1984). In 1960, after witnessing hunger in
West Virginia, John F. Kennedy made the eradication of hunger one of his
campaign promises. His pilot food stamp program became, as a result of
the passage of The Food Stamp Act of 1964, a national food assistance
program. The purpose of this law, was to aid low income families in
improving their diets and overall nutritional status.

In 1968, hunger resurfaced as a national political issue. This time,
however, studies were undertaken by various groups to document the
existence of this problem. The Citizens' Board of Inquiry into Hunger and
Malnutrition in the United States [Citizens' Board of Inquiry] documented
256 counties in the U.S. that required emergency food assistance for its
low income recipients. As a result of this and other studies, a special
Senate committee was formed and a 1969 White House conference was

convened. In the early 1970s existing food assistance programs were expanded and new programs initiated. In a 1977 report to the Senate Select Committee on Nutrition and Human Needs, government food assistance programs were heralded as the catalysts for the virtual eradication of hunger in the United States (U.S. Senate 1977).

One of the issues that emerged from the furor over hunger was an expressed need for systematic surveillance and monitoring of the nutritional status of the U.S. population. One resulting effort was the Ten-State Nutrition Survey — the first effort to assess the nutritional status of the U.S. population (USDHHS 1989). Since then, a variety of surveillance data, including that from the National Health and Nutrition Examination Survey [NHANES] series, have been collected (USDHHS 1989). Despite these surveillance efforts and the apparent recurrence of the hunger problem, the National Nutrition Monitoring System [NNMS] has failed to initiate data collection that would not only estimate the number and characteristics of hungry individuals, but would also do so in a timely fashion. In 1990, Public Law 101-445, The National Nutrition Monitoring and Related Research Act, was signed into law. This law mandates the sampling of low income population subsets on a continuous basis. These population subsets will be monitored for food expenditures and participation in food assistance programs. The government will also attempt to measure time periods in which the acquisition of adequate food is impaired due to insufficient monetary resources (U.S. Congress 1990).

The impact of the lack of adequate monitoring and surveillance in the 1980s is evidenced by the paucity of appropriate data with which to examine the hunger issue (Brown 1984). The importance of an accurate database for use in making informed policy decisions is acknowledged by policy planners (Hanft 1981; Bazzoli 1985). Health policy decisions are predicated upon epidemiologic databases (Ibrahim 1985) and policy formulation is hindered if not obstructed by inaccurate or nonexistent data.

The need for an accurate description of populations at risk of hunger is widely recognized by individuals conducting hunger research (Physician Task Force 1985). As noted previously, hundreds of studies were undertaken in an effort to assess the hunger problem in the U.S. Nestle and Guttmacher (1989) chose 25 of the state studies for comparison. The Physician Task Force presented a narrative summation of selected studies in its 1985 report: *Hunger in America*. Little effort was made, prior to this book, to integrate data from various studies or to merge and analyze data from surveys.

In this investigation, meta-analysis was employed to systematically examine studies in which survey methodology was utilized to study the hunger issue. Data from this analysis were synthesized in order to generate descriptive characteristics and baseline information about hunger survey respondents. Correlational analyses between certain socio-demographic characteristics and self-reported hunger were conducted. Measurement, surveillance, and monitoring techniques for the study of hungry people in the United States were discussed. Meta-analysis as a tool for investigating nonexperimental studies was evaluated. Finally, government food assistance programs during the decade of the 1980s and factors that were found to be critically linked to hunger were discussed.

STATEMENT OF THE PROBLEM

Adequate nutrition is a basic component of health. Reports, in the 1980s, indicated that the health of segments of the population of the United States was being compromised due to inadequate dietary intakes (Brown and Allen 1988). Conflicting evidence, however, as to the nature and extent of the problem and a failure by the U.S. government to establish a surveillance and monitoring system to appropriately measure the nutritional status of the nation resulted in a lack of government data to study the problem.

The purposes of this study were to establish consensus data regarding the characteristics of individuals who self-reported hunger, to make suggestions as to how this information can and should be collected in the future, and to discuss the policy implications of the research. This was accomplished through the examination of hunger surveys conducted in the U.S. between 1981 and 1989. During this time frame, a large number of hunger studies were conducted by states, churches, and private agencies. Meta-analysis was employed for the review of these hunger studies.

Meta-analysis is a methodological technique that is achieving importance in the field of health. For the most part, meta-analysis has been used to study the results from experimental research. Recently, however, this technique has gained favor with investigators studying survey research (Hall and Dornan 1990). This study, then, also provided information regarding the use of meta-analysis to study survey methodology.

RESEARCH QUESTIONS

1. What are the characteristics of individuals who sought emergency food assistance?

   a) What are the basic socio-demographic characteristics of individuals who sought emergency food assistance?

   b) Do these characteristics vary depending on the type of food assistance facility or the type of survey administered?

2. To what degree are each of the following factors correlated with hunger and are there interactions between some of the factors?

   a. Gender/sex
   b. Ethnicity
   c. Age
   d. Marital status
   e. Education
   f. Employment status
   g. Income level
   h. Income source
   I. Household size
   j. Household composition
   k. Special dietary needs
   l. Food stamp participation
   m. Participation in government food assistance programs
   n. Participation in government assistance programs
   o. Living conditions
   p. Geographic location
   q. Type of locale

3. What recommendations can be made for future meta-analytic investigations of survey research?

4. What are the policy implications of the research findings?

    a) What conclusions about government food assistance policy in the 1980s can be drawn from the results of this study?

    b) How can information from this study be used to aid in future policy decisions?

ORGANIZATION OF THE BOOK

Chapters two through seven are organized in the following manner. The second chapter is a review of the background literature related to the study of hunger in the 1980s. This chapter contains a brief discussion of the physiological effects of insufficient caloric intake and adverse consequences for certain at-risk populations in the United States. An examination of the history of hunger reports and the response of the U.S. citizenry and government is also undertaken in this chapter. The final section in this chapter involves the methods used to monitor hunger in the U.S. and the National Nutrition Monitoring System. Meta-analysis was used to assist in the systematic review of hunger studies conducted in the United States in the 1980s and Chapter Three provides an overview of this method of investigation. From there, an extensive discussion of the data collection and the process used to select the surveys used for statistical analysis is undertaken. Chapter Four contains a discussion of the statistical analyses employed in the study. This chapter contains information about the socio-demographic characteristics of the survey respondents as well as the results of the correlational analyses. Chapter Five is a discussion of the use of meta-analysis in a study of surveys. The focus of Chapter Six is an examination of food assistance policy in the United States. This analysis is drawn from a perspective gained by studying the quantitative and qualitative results of the analysis of the studies. The seventh and final chapter contains conclusions and recommendations for surveillance and monitoring of hunger in the United States, improvement of future hunger surveys, and suggestions for food assistance policy in the U.S.

II

Literature Review

In this chapter, three areas that are integral to a thorough investigation of hunger in the United States are examined. First, the effects of hunger and malnutrition on human beings are discussed. The health consequences of hunger are discussed in terms of specific populations (e.g., pregnant women) that are particularly susceptible to negative health effects of malnutrition. Second, a brief historical recountal of the history of hunger and food assistance in the United States is presented. Finally, the history of hunger surveys, types of hunger surveys conducted in the decade of the 1980s, and the National Nutrition Monitoring System is discussed.

HUNGER, MALNUTRITION, AND HUMAN HEALTH

Food is the basic sustenance for human life. In the strictest biochemical sense, food is necessary for three basic functions in the human body: 1) it provides for maintenance of the bodily functions; 2) it provides necessary energy; and 3) it is required for the replacement of tissue (Rolfes, DeBruyne, and Whitney 1990). Food also provides nurture and is a psychological component in human development (Guthrie 1979; Robinson et al. 1986). Many cultural or social customs also place importance on food. When food is unobtainable in adequate amounts or there is an imbalance in the intake of essential nutrients, the health of the individual is threatened.

Hunger and Malnutrition Terminology

In order to discuss hunger and malnutrition, it is necessary to agree on the terminology to be used. For the purposes of this study, the following terms were utilized:

Starvation. Starvation is the condition in which the individual is dying from lack of food (Robinson et al. 1986).

Undernutrition. Undernutrition occurs when an individual consumes an inadequate amount of kilocalories and/or essential nutrients (protein, vitamins, minerals, and water) (Robinson et al. 1986).

Malnutrition. Malnutrition literally means bad or poor nutrition. Malnutrition exists when an individual fails to obtain the essential nutrients in proper quantity or proportions. Malnutrition, therefore, results in impaired health, growth, and/or physiologic functioning. It is also associated with increased risk for impaired psychologic health. It should be noted that malnutrition is not always characterized by a deficiency of nutrients, but can occur when nutrients are ingested in excessive quantities (Brown 1990).

Protein-calorie malnutrition (PCM). Protein-calorie malnutrition is malnourishment that occurs because the diet of an individual is deficient in protein and/or calories. It is sometimes referred to as protein-energy malnutrition (PEM) (Jelliffe and Jelliffe 1989).

Kwashiorkor. Kwashiorkor is a type of PCM. It results when the inadequate diet has relatively more calories than protein. Edema, skin lesions, loss of pigmentation in the hair, muscle wasting, moon face, failure to grow, hypoproteinemia, and psychomotor changes are all characteristic signs of kwashiorkor (Jelliffe and Jelliffe 1989).

Marasmus. Marasmus is the second type of PCM and is the result of severe undernutrition. In this disease there is an overall lack of both protein and calories. It can occur in adults, but is most commonly seen in young children. The disease is characterized by severe growth retardation and wasting of muscle and subcutaneous fat (Jelliffe and Jelliffe 1989).

Hunger. Hunger can be defined as acute physiologic hunger or as chronic hunger. Acute physiologic hunger is best described as a sensation or strong desire for food. Chronic hunger refers to a prolonged condition in which insufficient nutrient intake occurs (Jelliffe and Jelliffe 1989). Chronic hunger exists when an individual experiences difficulties in obtaining adequate amounts of food. This can occur for a variety of reasons including lack of income, lack of access to food, and lack of cooking facilities (FRAC 1984).

Health Effects of Hunger and Malnutrition

Protein-calorie malnutrition is a type of malnutrition that is found mainly in some poorer, developing countries (Brown 1990). Although the PCM diseases of marasmus and kwashiorkor are rarely seen in developed nations, they have been reported in the United States (Listernick et al. 1985; Physician Task Force 1985; Brown and Allen 1988). The occurrence of these cases in the U.S. makes them relevant to this study.

There is a large body of information pertaining to the physiological effects of chronic protein-calorie malnutrition. The most commonly discussed diseases, in terms of malnourishment, are marasmus and kwashiorkor. Protein-calorie malnutrition during the prenatal period is characterized by poor outcome including elevated morbidity and mortality and intrauterine growth retardation (Jelliffe and Jelliffe 1989). Because of a low caloric intake during the first years of life, severely malnourished children are often extremely small and have shortened life expectancy (Jelliffe and Jelliffe 1989; National Academy of Sciences [NAS] 1990). Growth retarded or low birth weight babies are also at an increased risk for mortality during the neonatal and post-neonatal periods (McCormick 1985).

Other types of primary malnutrition include the deficiency diseases. These occur when a particular micronutrient or, in most cases, multiple micronutrients, are present in less than adequate amounts in the diet. An example of a micronutrient deficiency disease is scurvy which is caused by a diet deficient in ascorbic acid.

Secondary malnutrition is a type of malnutrition associated with disease and is associated with altered absorption, metabolism, storage, and excretion (Brown 1990). In secondary malnutrition, the nutritional problem is not caused by dietary intake. Rather, there is a condition or disease that is causing a problem with the proper assimilation of the micronutrient. Gastrointestinal-tract illness (e.g., diarrhea) is an example of a disease that can cause secondary malnutrition (Brown 1990).

Hunger and Malnutrition Among High-Risk Groups

Certain groups of individuals are at an increased risk for malnutrition. Pregnant women, infants and children, and the elderly have the highest risk for malnutrition due to their increased nutritional requirements. This risk is exacerbated when income is low (USDHHS 1988). The following is an examination of the nutritional problems that affect these high-risk groups.

Pregnant women. The prenatal period is a time of increased nutritional need due to the demands of pregnancy coupled with the woman's normal physiologic requirements (Brown 1990; NAS 1990). Adequate nutrition of the mother is important to optimize a pregnancy outcome. Chronic malnutrition during the prenatal period has been linked to a poor pregnancy outcome (Jelliffe and Jelliffe 1989). Women who begin pregnancy with poor nutritional status have higher health risks for both themselves and the unborn fetus, than do women who enter pregnancy in good nutritional condition (NAS 1990).

Females with decreased iron reserves prior to conception, have an increased risk of anemia (Dawson and McGanity 1987). Increased stress on iron stores during gestation heightens the possibility of anemia (Dallman, Yip, and Johnson 1984). The most common nutrient deficiency among pregnant women in the U.S. is iron deficiency (Brown 1990). Researchers using data from NHANES II have estimated that 5-14% of females in the 15-44 year age group have impaired iron status (Life Sciences Research Office 1985).

Megaloblastic anemia can also be a problem during pregnancy, although it is infrequently seen in the United States (Rolfes, DeBruyne, and Whitney 1990). The diets of pregnant women seldom meet the increased folic acid requirement (Brown 1990). Since folate is vital to many metabolic processes (including the metabolism of several amino acids) a deficiency of this micronutrient in the early stages of pregnancy could result in low birth weight, malformations, and spontaneous abortion (Rolfes, DeBruyne, and Whitney 1990).

Energy stores prior to conception may also play an important role in fetal development. Prepregnancy weight-for-height is an important factor in birth outcome (NAS 1990). Nutritional interventions that increase the weight of the female prior to conception may increase the birth weight of the baby (Rolfes, DeBruyne, and Whitney 1990). This suggests that supplementation of the maternal diet should occur prior to conception in order to increase the probability of optimally-sized, healthy babies. Smaller than average females have a greater chance of giving birth to a low birth weight baby than do normally or above average-sized females (Robinson et al. 1986; NAS 1990). Providing supplementation to females in their growth years would, if genetically predisposed to do so, produce women of a larger size. This in turn, would increase the chance of normal weight babies (Lechtig et al. 1979).

There are also risks for the growing fetus when the mother is poorly nourished during the prenatal period. The fetus requires a diet rich in protein, vitamins, and minerals in order to insure the proper development of vital tissues and organs. Miscarriage, stillbirth, and abnormal fetal development, have been linked to severe malnutrition during pregnancy in experimental animals and World War II starvation studies (Winick 1979). Researchers note that there is some evidence to suggest that low dietary intake or deficiencies of some vitamins and minerals can also have an adverse effect on a fetal outcome (NAS 1990). Energy supplementation during the prenatal period has been found to have a positive effect on birth size in some studies (Institute of Medicine [IOM] 1985).

When malnourished populations received prenatal energy supplementation, the percentage of low birth weight babies dropped (NAS 1990). However, when females were more well-nourished there was little change in the proportion of low birth weight infants (NAS 1990). The greater the malnourishment of the mother, the more dramatic the effects of energy supplementation. Fetal growth is associated with total gestational weight gain as well as the timing of weight gain during the three trimesters of pregnancy (Taffel and Keppel 1986). Lower net weight gains are also associated with an increased risk of intrauterine growth retardation and perinatal mortality (NAS 1990).

Recommendations for appropriate weight gain during pregnancy has been an important topic in medical circles. Based on recent evidence, researchers suggest that weight gain should be a function of prepregnancy weight for height. Thin women should gain more weight and heavy women should gain less (NAS 1990).

Low birth weight brings a plethora of possible problems to the newborn infant. In terms of survival, the infant's chances are severely diminished (IOM 1985). Low birth weight (less than 2500 grams) babies are less likely to survive during the first year of life than normal birth weight babies (McCormick 1985). Low birth weight babies have a thirty-times fold increase in mortality during the first year of life compared to normal weight babies (Physician Task Force 1985). Very low birth weight (less than 1500 grams) infants who are often premature (less than 37 weeks) have an even worse rate of survival (IOM 1985; Kleinman and Kessel 1987). These babies face health problems including immature lung development, hypoglycemia, hypocalcemia, and polycythemia. They are also at higher risk for long-term growth and development problems. Very low birth weight babies have an increased chance of mental and physical retardation (IOM 1985; McCormick 1985). Low birth weight babies surviving the postneonatal period are 50% more likely to possess serious illness or developmental problems (Shapiro et al. 1980). There is a high correlation between intrauterine growth retardation, and failure to perform well in school (Physician Task Force 1985).

Researchers have recently revealed the positive impact on a pregnancy outcome of nutritional supplementation among pregnant females (Rush et al. 1988; Hediger et al. 1989). Female participants in the Special Supplemental Program for Women, Infants, and Children (WIC) exhibited an increase in weight gain during pregnancy. Participation in the WIC program has been associated with an increase in mean birth weight (i.e., a decrease in the number of low birth weight babies born) (Stockbauer 1986; Rush et al. 1988; Avruch and Cackley 1995). Kotelchuck et al. (1984) found an association between participation in the WIC program and decreased neonatal mortality. The research of Buescher et al. (1993) led them to estimate that for each $1.00 spent on WIC services, Medicaid savings was $2.91.

Infants and children. The infant mortality rate is a key indicator of the health status of a nation. Despite recent improvements, the United States still has a poor ranking among other developed countries. The U.S. ranks twenty-fourth compared to other industrialized nations and had an infant mortality rate of 6.9% for white mothers (USDHHS 1995). This rate is significantly higher for members of minority groups. Among Black females, for instance, the infant mortality rate is 16.8% (USDHHS 1995). The risk of mortality for black infants, then, is 2.2 times higher for Black infants than for white infants (Singh and Yu 1995). Although hunger and malnutrition are not the only causes of this elevated infant mortality rate, they are important factors (Brown 1987).

Infants and children represent a very high risk group for malnutrition and its related sequelae. The first year of life is a time of such rapid growth that it is unmatched at any other time in the postnatal life cycle (Brown 1990). Infants who do not receive enough calories during this period of time have their energy channeled into daily maintenance of bodily functions rather than cellular growth. Acute periods of PCM result in a variety of physiologic effects and growth deficits such as wasting (Waterlow 1972), while chronic malnutrition during critical periods may result in irreparable stunting (Jelliffe and Jelliffe 1989). Apathy, listlessness, loss of ability to concentrate, behavioral problems, slowed learning, and comprehension have all been attributed to an insufficient intake of kilocalories, protein, iron, and other nutrients in children (Connecticut Association for Human Services 1986; Jelliffe and Jelliffe 1989).

Most brain development occurs during the prenatal period and the first two years of postnatal life (Kramer et al. 1989; Brown 1990). Head circumference (used as an indicator of normal brain growth) and intellectual development are frequently curtailed in children with PCM (Winick 1979; Jelliffe and Jelliffe 1989). Since head circumference is largely determined during the first two years of life, adequate nutrition is of significant importance at this time (Brown 1990). Findings indicate that children who are subjected to severe and long-term deficits of energy, protein, and other nutrients appear to have limited intellectual development (Winick 1979; Brown 1990). In a longitudinal study conducted by Freeman et al. (1977) it was found that children receiving a higher caloric supplement were more likely to score high in cognitive performance than children who did not receive the supplement. This supports other studies that indicate a link between nutrition and cognitive development (Brown 1979;1990).

There is some evidence that an adequate energy intake in infancy and childhood is important for later social-emotional development (Barrett, Radke-Yarrow, and Klein 1982). Iron deficiency has been linked to reduced growth velocity and increased morbidity risk (Chwang, Soemantri, and Pollitt 1988), as well as behavioral alterations. Oski, Honig, Helu, and Howanitz (1982) concluded that iron deficiency, even in the absence of clinical anemia, results in biochemical alterations that impair behavior in infants. Although the behavioral consequences of malnutrition are not well understood, malnourished infants may have reduced social responsiveness, impaired attentional processes, heightened irritability, an inability to tolerate frustration, low activity levels, and reduced independence (Haas and Fairchild 1989). Barrett, Radke-Yarrow, and Klein (1982) found that adequate energy intake in infancy was a significant predictor of future normal social-emotional development. Galler and Ramsey (1989) found significant behavioral disorders including the inability to concentrate among a previously malnourished school-age population. Pollitt and Leibel (1976) found that iron deficiency affects cognitive function. Pollitt, Leibel, and Greenfield (1991) suggested that poor health and malnutrition may have an effect on a child's ability to learn.

Malnutrition in children has been associated with an increased risk of disease and infection (Physician Task Force 1985; Robinson et al. 1986). Although it varies from individual to individual, researchers have found the existence of a synergistic relationship between malnutrition and infection (Chandra 1991). Infection can cause decreased food ingestion by decreasing appetite and altering nutrient transport, metabolism, and excretion rates. In addition, the presence of diarrhea associated with infection can cause decreased nutrient absorption (Chandra 1983; 1991).

Failure to thrive (FTT) is a syndrome that involves significant growth and developmental delay. Failure to thrive syndrome occurs when a child is at or below the 15th percentile of the median weight for age (Polhamus, Peterson, and Miller 1989). Lack of proper nutrition has been associated with failure to thrive (Physician Task Force 1985). Polhamus, Peterson, and Miller (1989) found that while history of low birth weight and prematurity constituted high biological risk factors, poverty was a major psychosocial risk factor for FTT.

Elderly. Old age is a time of heightened nutritional risk (USDHHS 1988; Goodwin 1989; Posner et al. 1994). Research indicates that the elderly (over age 65) are, as compared with other age groups, relatively uninformed about good nutritional practices (Minkler 1984). Furthermore, poverty is an important environmental determinant of inadequate nutrition in the elderly population (Posner et al. 1994). Inadequate energy and calcium intake levels present problems in this age group. In NHANES I, only 50% of the elderly population had energy intakes that met 67% of the National Research Council [NRC] recommendations (USDHHS 1988). Mean calcium intakes in NHANES I were found to be below the Recommended Dietary Allowances [RDA] for both women and men in the over 65 age group (USDHHS 1988). Iron, vitamins A and C, protein, and niacin deficiencies also pose a problem for many elderly people (Franz 1981).

Advancing age, and its related physiologic and behavioral changes, diminishes the need for some nutrients while increasing the need for others. Many elderly are not particularly successful at achieving the proper nutritional balance in their diets. Factors such as lack of food, poor socioeconomic status, lack of nutrition knowledge, lack of interest in cooking, lack of mobility, loss of senses, cognitive and behavioral changes, increase the risk for nutritional problems in the elderly population. This lack of proper nutrition often results in or exacerbates disease. Shannon, Smiciklas-Wright, Davis and Lewis (1983) suggested that increased risk for chronic disease and illness in the elderly is partially related to poor nutritional practices. In fact, it is estimated that 85% of older persons living outside of institutional settings have one or more chronic conditions that would be improved with appropriate nutrition (Posner et al. 1993).

Malnutrition in this population can have dire consequences. The elderly are at heightened risk for infection due to a general decline in immunocompetence status. Malnutrition increases the susceptibility to infection (USDHHS 1988; Chandra 1991). Physiologic changes and some common medical conditions of the elderly impair digestion or absorption of nutrients making the need for nutrient-dense foods critically important (Weimer 1983). Aging is often associated with decline in food intake due to decreased activity and appetite. Diets with low nutrient density increase the risk for malnutrition (Wolinsky et al. 1985). The elderly have a high incidence of chronic diseases associated with or aggravated by nutrient deficiencies. This phenomenon increases the requirements for certain nutrients (USDHHS 1988). Eighty-five percent of the individuals over age 65 have at least one chronic disease or disability (Physician Task Force 1985). This can result in increased use of medication and increased hospitalization.

Low income. Low income populations have been identified as being at nutritional risk (NAS 1990). Overnutrition or undernutrition exists at most income levels, yet, members of low income populations are at the greatest overall nutritional risk (Kleinman and Kessel 1987; Jelliffe and Jelliffe 1989). Iron deficiency, for example, is most often found in members of lower socioeconomic groups (NAS 1990; Pollitt 1994).

Poor families spend a larger proportion of their income on food than families in higher socioeconomic groups, but have diets that are often nutritionally inadequate (Kinsey 1994). Emmons (1986) found that low income groups generally had inadequate food and nutrient supply. Whole grain cereals and green leafy vegetables were noticeably lacking. Patterson and Block (1988) found that consumption of fruits and vegetables increased with income. Recently, researchers have cited evidence that suggests that grains, vegetables, and fruit in the diet may prevent major chronic diseases such as cancer, cardiovascular disease, and diabetes (USDHHS 1988).

Current morbidity and mortality statistics show a disproportionately higher incidence of the nutritionally related diseases of obesity, hypertension, diabetes, cardiovascular diseases, pneumonia, and influenza among members of low income groups (Wegman 1985). Increased risk for these conditions has been linked with lifetime nutritional inadequacy (USDHHS 1988). Iron-deficiency anemia in the United States is high among low income children compared to children in other income groups (Pollitt 1994).

Mild malnutrition can also affect young and middle-aged adults. Malnourished individuals may exhibit a loss of productivity at work and/or impaired social function (Physician Task Force 1985). Primary malnutrition can result in deficiency diseases (Brown 1990) and may impair immunologic function thus resulting in increased rates of infection (Chandra 1991).

Summary

Chronic hunger caused by an inability to obtain food in constant, adequate supply is different from the physiologic sensation of hunger. Severe types of protein-calorie malnutrition associated with chronic hunger, such as marasmus and kwashiorkor, are rarely seen in developed nations. In the 1980s, however, cases of these types of PCM were reported in the United States.

A chronic insufficient intake of energy and protein is a particular problem in certain groups of individuals, including pregnant women. Poor nutritional status prior to and during pregnancy can have a negative impact on pregnancy outcome. Good nutritional status may reduce the risk of low birth weight babies. Low birth weight babies have a lower rate of survival than optimally-sized infants.

Children and infants not receiving an adequate, constant supply of nutrients may experience a reduction in brain growth, weight, height, and cognitive skills, as well as being more at risk for apathy and listlessness. Increased risk for disease and infection also can occur in children who are malnourished.

Lack of proper nutrition in the elderly may result in aggravation of existing health problems and an increased risk of infection. A variety of chronic conditions that impair digestion and absorption occur in elderly individuals. Consumption of a nutrient dense and balanced diet is especially important in elderly people in order to minimize nutritional and other health risks.

Low income families spend a larger proportion of their income on food than higher income families. Low income families are at increased risk for malnutrition due to the fact that obtaining adequate food is difficult because of lack of money and lack of access to a variety of higher-quality, more nutrient-dense foodstuffs. Researchers have shown that consumption of fresh fruits and vegetables increases as a function of increasing income. Furthermore, the consumption of fresh fruits and vegetables has been associated with the prevention of some chronic illnesses.

HISTORY OF HUNGER AND FOOD ASSISTANCE IN THE UNITED STATES

This section outlines major influences that have shaped the formulation of food assistance programs in the United States. The formulation of food assistance programs is presented and discussed in their historical import.

Colonial Period to the Great Depression (1620-1929)

Occurrences of hunger in the United States have been reported since the arrival of the first European settlers. In fact, the first reports of recorded hunger in the New World occurred during the "starving time" of 1620-1621 at Plymouth. The Pilgrims arrived in Plymouth at the onset of winter. There they weathered out the first year by surviving on what few supplies they had brought with them and, as legend has it, the help of the

American Indian, Squanto (Bradford 1953).

As time progressed, the Pilgrims, taught by local indigenous peoples, learned to work the soil and provide for their own sustenance. Until the latter part of the eighteenth century, the United States was a predominantly agrarian state. Families worked the land to provide for their own sustenance. Hunger, because of its direct connection with physical labor, was viewed as something that happened to a lazy or ill-prepared individual. The Protestant Work Ethic was deeply rooted in the citizenry of the United States (Bremner 1988). After the Civil War, industrialism gained a foothold in the United States. As the population began to shift from rural to urban, hunger became more of a concern. The urban residents had no way of obtaining food directly from the soil. The hungry had to rely, as had the Pilgrims, on the generosity of others. The churches and various philanthropic agencies had the responsibility of feeding the hungry (Hunter 1904; Bremner 1988). During the 1930s, however, certain events changed the way in which the United States dealt with hunger and poverty.

The New Deal and World War II (1930-1942)

The economic depression of the 1930s brought widespread unemployment, poverty, and hunger. During this era of the New Deal many activities traditionally accepted as private pursuits became the responsibilities of the federal government (Berry 1984). One of the most significant programs to emerge from this era was the surplus commodities program (Saloutos 1982).

Surplus commodities. The farm depression of the 1920s and the general economic depression of the 1930s had resulted in an extremely depressed farm economy. Farmers had stockpiled large quantities of surplus commodities and crop prices were depressed. The New Dealers believed that, because of an impending war in Europe, a loss in foreign markets would be imminent. In order to relieve farm surpluses and aid the farm economy, therefore, a direct distribution of surplus commodities to consumers was adopted (DeVault and Pitts 1984). The government would purchase surplus commodities from farmers and, then, distribute this food to unemployed, indigent Americans (Schapsmeier and Schapsmeier 1975).

The major impetus for this legislation, however, was not to avert starvation, but, rather, to ensure higher farm prices (DeVault and Pitts 1984).

Problems with the surplus commodities program began almost immediately. The federal government received complaints of waste (because some families received too much food) and complaints of misuse and fraud (because some families were giving away or selling food). It was virtually impossible to gauge whether or not needy individuals were receiving the food (United States House of Representatives [USHR] 1976). Furthermore, grocers and retailers were disgruntled because the system of distribution bypassed them and, therefore, they did not benefit economically.

Food Stamp Plan. By the late 1930s the need for a revision in the distribution system was apparent. Eventually, the idea of food stamps emerged. Under the "pilot" food stamp plan, families on relief purchased orange-colored stamps. These orange stamps were worth face value and could be used on any food item available for purchase in any participating grocery store. For every $1.00 in orange stamps purchased, recipients were given 50 cents worth of blue stamps. The blue stamps were used to purchase food items designated as surplus by the Secretary of Agriculture. The theory (and hope) was that the poor would spend the same dollar amount on food with the orange stamps and that the purchase of food with the blue stamps would serve to increase the amount of food they actually brought home (Berry 1984). Then Secretary of Agriculture Wallace was enthusiastic about the program. He believed that the food stamp plan would increase the consumption of farm products (which would help agriculture), provide more and better food for low income families (which would improve public health), and help business by having more merchandise move through the channels of trade (USHR 1976).

On May 16, 1939, the first food stamps were purchased in Rochester, New York. The program ran until March 1, 1943 when the food stamp program was terminated. World War II ended all talk of hunger in the United States' population. Americans sent surplus food supplies to troops and starving allies. Upon termination of the food stamp program, then Secretary of Agriculture Claud Wickard declared the food stamp program successful and expressed his belief that the program would be used in the future (USHR 1976).

At the peak of the food stamp program, four million people in selected areas of the country had been served (Congressional Budget Office [CBO]

1977). Every aspect of the food stamp program was not favorable, however. During the almost four year run of the food stamp program certain problems emerged and these same difficulties would also plague future food stamp programs.

One major problem that afflicted the program was non-participation by eligible recipients. Lack of understanding of the program and inability to purchase the minimal amount of orange stamps were cited as the main reasons for non-participation (USHR 1976). The second major problem posed to the program was ensuring compliance with regulations. Although, possible violations by consumers and retailers were recognized as threats to future funding of the food stamp program, there was no method to assess the degree of fraud or non-participation in the food stamp programs of the 1940s. Estimates varied as to the nature and extent of the fraud. On May 5, 1942, the Department of Agriculture issued new regulations to prevent violations, however, the food stamp program was terminated before the effect of these new regulations could be evaluated.

In spite of the problems of the food stamp program many legislators believed that terminating the food stamp program was a mistake (Berry 1984). World War II had brought information about the nutritional status of the U.S. population to the attention of the legislature. Forty percent of the men selected for active duty in the armed services were rejected for health reasons. Many of these men suffered from malnutrition (Physician Task Force 1985). Immediately after the food stamp program was terminated, in 1943, two bills were introduced to establish a food stamp program through public law. The previous program had never been explicitly authorized by Congress. A series of bills providing for a food stamp program were introduced from 1943–1964. Each of these bills was defeated.

School Lunch Program. The second major food program established by the U.S. government evolved during World War II. It became clear during this time period, that a significant portion of the U.S. population was malnourished. As noted previously, 40% of all draftees were rejected for military service because of poor health. The Surgeon General reported that 70% of the young men, who had experienced poor nutrition during the depression, were rejected from military service (FRAC 1984). The issue of proper nutrition then became a national security concern. In 1946, Congress passed the National School Lunch Act. Its purpose, as expressed by Congress, was to protect the health and welfare of the children of the United States. This was to be accomplished by establishing a nonprofit

School Lunch Program. Low income students would be provided with a nutritious lunch. This food assistance program also provided for the use of agricultural surplus commodities. Thus, ensuring, as had the food stamp program, that the interests of agriculture would be protected (FRAC 1984). No other major food programs were initiated between 1946 and 1961.

The Kennedy Years and Johnson's War on Poverty (1961-1966)

In the late 1950s, John F. Kennedy witnessed hunger while campaigning for the presidency. The hunger that he viewed while in West Virginia had a profound effect on him and he made hunger relief one of his campaign promises. In February 1961, President John F. Kennedy gave his first executive order in which he released government food surpluses to the needy of West Virginia (McGovern 1964). In addition to the release of surplus commodities, he inaugurated a pilot study food stamp program. In May 1961, regulations for the first food stamp program since 1943 were published in the *Federal Register*.

This pilot program varied in some respects to the previous food stamp program of the 1930s and 1940s. The blue stamp or surplus commodities component was eliminated. Food stamp program participants were, as before, required to purchase food stamps. Participants paid a reduced amount for food stamps of higher purchasing value. This difference in price represented the federal contribution.

Food Stamp Program. In 1963, President Kennedy, in his January 31 farm message, asked Congress to provide for a permanent food stamp program. The following year, President Lyndon B. Johnson, renewed this request for legislation to enact a permanent food stamp program as one of the steps in his declared "War on Poverty" (Egan 1994). After great deliberation, Public Law No. 88-525, The Food Stamp Act of 1964, was signed into law on August 31, 1964. The law established the Food Stamp Program as a permanent program designed to " . . . safeguard the health and well-being of the Nation's population and raise levels of nutrition among low income households." (U.S. Congress 1964, 42 U.S.C. 1782).

From 1964 to 1968 the Food Stamp Program operated, for the most part, as was written in the Food Stamp Act of 1964. Legislative action came primarily in the form of appropriations. This was a period of quiet growth for the Food Stamp Program. Participation rates increased as did the number of participating regions. Funding alone was the mechanism that controlled growth of the Food Stamp Program during these years (Berry 1984).

School Breakfast Program. The topic of hungry American citizens lay dormant for many years. In the mid-1960s, however, studies linking poor scholastic performance and poor nutritional status began to appear in the literature. Some reports documented that poor students and students from rural areas (who had to travel long distances to school) were not eating breakfast. When the Iowa Breakfast Studies showed a relationship between the lack of a nutritious breakfast and poor performance in school, Congress responded by signing the Child Nutrition Act of 1966 into law. This legislation provided for the pilot study for the School Breakfast Program.

Reports and Documentation of Hunger (1967-1969)

Amid widespread reports of hunger and malnutrition, government food assistance programs became the topic of scrutiny by Congress and advocacy by outside interest groups. Groups in both the private and public sectors scrambled to collect evidence regarding the extent of the hunger problem.

Senate Subcommittee on Employment, Manpower, and Poverty. In April of 1967, the Senate Subcommittee on Employment, Manpower, and Poverty held hearings in Jackson, Mississippi on the subjects of poverty and the Head Start Program. They were apprised of massive poverty and hunger in the region. Due to the testimonies given by some individuals, two of the four senators opted to stay another day in order to visit these impoverished people. This unscheduled tour of Delta homes gave Democratic Senators Robert F. Kennedy (New York) and Joseph Clark (Pennsylvania) a firsthand look at hunger (Leinwand 1985). This was a media event and the television crews brought a glimpse of hungry Americans into households across the U.S. Thus, the hunger problem received national attention.

There had been evidence of a hunger problem in the U.S. prior to this time. Congressman Joseph Resnick of New York had seen and reported hunger eighteen months before. In early 1966, members of a poor contingent from Mississippi had camped across from the White House in order to bring attention to their economic plight (Kotz 1969).

Field Foundation and The Citizens' Board of Inquiry. After their tour of Delta homes, Kennedy and Clark returned to Washington and urged Secretary of Agriculture Orville Freeman to seek emergency help for the hungry of Mississippi. Freeman immediately dispatched two aides to investigate the allegations of hunger in Mississippi. The Senate Subcommittee on Employment, Manpower, and Poverty began holding hearings on hunger and federal food assistance programs. This marked the first time that the federal food assistance programs had ever been discussed by a committee other than an agricultural committee (Kotz 1969).

After reading the reports about the Kennedy–Clark trip, Leslie Dunbar, director of the Field Foundation, launched a long-planned fact-finding mission on the topic of hunger in the United States (Kotz 1969). In 1968, the Field Foundation gathered a national team of doctors who examined the problem in Mississippi and other Southern states. They found evidence of chronic hunger and malnutrition in the United States.

In 1968 a coalition, The Citizens' Board of Inquiry into Hunger and Malnutrition in the United States, was formed. The objective of this coalition was to focus national attention on the issue of hunger (Kotz 1969). In its report "Hunger U.S.A.," this group revealed that, indeed, hunger and malnutrition existed in the United States. "Hunger U.S.A." charged that millions of Americans were affected by hunger and malnutrition and that the severity and extent of the problem were increasing every year. The report recommended the enactment of massive changes in the Food Stamp Program and the formation of other food assistance programs in order to alleviate the hunger problem. The Citizens' Board of Inquiry suggested providing food stamps and/or commodity distribution to every county in the United States. Furthermore, this report recommended the simplification of eligibility procedures and free food stamps for families with no cash. According to The Citizens' Board of Inquiry, many of the purchase prices were set too high and needed to be lowered in order to encourage participation in the Food Stamp Program. The Citizens' Board of Inquiry classified 256 counties in the U.S. as "hunger counties" that required immediate emergency assistance. A hunger county was defined as one in which poverty is high (more than 25% of the population) and food assistance is low (less than 33% of the eligible poor are receiving food assistance) (Physician Task Force 1986). The report identified only rural counties in the Southeast and Southwest and not any urban ghettoes.

Senate Select Committee on Nutrition and Human Needs. The day after "Hunger U.S.A." was released, Senator George S. McGovern (who had been the first director of Food for Peace, a program designed to send food to other countries) proposed the formation of the Senate Select Committee on Nutrition and Human Needs. The thirteen member committee was purely investigative and had no authority to draft legislation (Berry 1984). The Senate Select Committee on Nutrition and Human Needs examined the issue of hunger and malnutrition in the United States. In the report of their findings, Committee members stated that the "War on Poverty" declared in 1964 had failed to recognize the problem of hunger in the United States and the health effects of malnutrition.

The Committee observed that clinical cases of malnutrition existed in America and that low income families, infants, and preschool children represented groups in which acute health problems associated with malnutrition existed. Kwashiorkor and marasmus were documented in the poorest sections of the Nation. The Committee stated that hunger and malnutrition can have an adverse effect on physical and mental development of a young child and that the emotional and psychological effects of hunger on individuals and groups cannot be calculated (Berry 1984). Malnutrition, the Committee observed, is a cause and result of ill-health. Furthermore, malnutrition increases the chance of infection, may prolong illness, and malnourished individuals may be subjected to more serious diseases. The major reason for malnutrition and hunger in the United States was, according to the Committee, lack of money.

The Senate Select Committee stated that the two major food assistance programs (surplus commodities and food stamps) had been inadequate. Many individuals in need of assistance were not being served. Many participants did not receive enough food to meet minimal nutritional needs. The Senate Select Committee reported a failure of the food assistance programs. This was due, charged the Committee, to improper funding and administration of these programs.

In December of 1969, President Nixon convened the White House Conference on Hunger. The conference members concluded that ten to fifteen million Americans were hungry and another ten million were in need of help. Although many anti-hunger advocates argued for a simple cash stipend to the needy, the authors of the report recommended enhancing existing food assistance programs (DeVault and Pitts 1984). In subsequent years, it became the goal of the Nixon administration to eradicate the problem of hunger in the U.S. (Kotz 1969).

Efforts to Alleviate the Hunger Problem (1970-1972)

As a result of information on the incidence of the problem collected by the Senate Select Committee on Nutrition and Human Needs, the White House Conference on Hunger, The Ten-State Nutrition survey and a number of other hunger studies, legislators passed a wide variety of legislation designed to ameliorate the hunger problem in the United States.

Food stamps. The first major amendments to the Food Stamp Act of 1964 were enacted by Congress in late 1970 and became Public Law No. 91-671 on January 11, 1971. This legislation increased food stamp appropriations and expanded eligibility and geographic coverage. From this point forward, food stamp allotments would be annually indexed to the rate of food-price inflation. Eligibility standards would be removed from state-control and would be federally established. Puerto Rico, Guam, and the Virgin Islands were also declared eligible to participate in the Food Stamp Program.

Children. In 1972 an amendment was made to the Child Nutrition Act of 1966. Public Law 92-433 authorized the establishment of the Special Supplemental Women, Infant, and Children program as a two-year pilot program. During this time the School Lunch and School Breakfast programs were expanded. The Summer Food Program for children was also revised and expanded (FRAC 1984).

Elderly. Two major programs for the elderly were established in 1972. In that year Congress amended the Older Americans Act of 1965 and established the Congregate Meals Program and the Home Delivered Meals Program (commonly known as "Meals on Wheels"). Meals on Wheels provides the opportunity for needy individuals over age 60 to obtain at least one nutritious meal a day (Wisconsin Nutrition Project 1984).

The "Decline" of Hunger (1972-1977)

In 1972, Department of Agriculture Assistant Secretary Richard Lyng, announced that the job of feeding the hungry in the U.S. had been accomplished because virtually all indigent families had access to federal food assistance programs. His pronouncement, however, was premature. An examination by the U.S. Senate Select Committee on Nutrition and Human Needs found 263 hunger counties in the Nation (Physician Task Force 1985). During the years between 1972 and 1977, Congress acted to expand existing food assistance programs.

In 1977 a team of physicians returned to the regions in which serious malnutrition and hunger had been observed a decade before. Even though the pockets of poverty still existed, the physicians noted that hunger and malnutrition were significantly reduced (Physician Task Force 1985). By 1977, for the most part, the hunger that Senator Robert Kennedy had reported in April of 1967 had disappeared. In 1977 the Senate Select Committee on Nutrition and Human Needs reported tremendous advances in overcoming the hunger problem in the United States. Hunger, they concluded, no longer existed in the U.S. to any great degree (U.S. Senate 1977). Also, in this year, the Senate Select Committee on Hunger and Human Needs was disbanded during a committee restructuring in Congress.

Legislative Changes and the Reappearance of Hunger (1980-1982)

The beginning of the decade of the 1980s was a time of increased legislative activity for the Food Stamp Program. Legislation in the Food Stamp Program in the late 1970s had been confined to cuts in eligibility and benefits (FRAC 1984). In 1981, President Ronald Reagan signed the Omnibus Reconciliation Act of 1981 into law. The law provided for several cost-saving measures including: 1) the initial month's allotment of food stamps would be prorated from the date of application; 2) the timing of the annual adjustments in the cost of the thrifty food plan would be delayed and changed; 3) strikers who were not already eligible for food stamps would be ineligible; and 4) the Commonwealth of Puerto Rico would receive its food stamps in block grant form. In other legislation passed in 1981, Title XIII of the Agriculture and Food Act of 1981 (Public

Law No. 97-98) eliminated any inflation adjustment in food stamp benefits during fiscal 1982. The indexing period would be for 21 months ending June 30, 1982. After that, indexing would occur annually.

The Omnibus Reconciliation Act of 1982 also provided for cost-saving measures. Although the reforms outlined in this law did not save as much money as did the reforms of the Omnibus Reconciliation Act of 1981, the changes were estimated to save 1.9 billion dollars over three years. Changes in the Food Stamp Program were targeted at slowing the rate of growth of the program (USHR 1985b). The Omnibus Reconciliation Act of 1982 also reauthorized the Food Stamp Program for an additional three year period. Funding was set at 11.3 billion dollars for 1983.

An interesting addition to legislation in this year was the insistence of Congress that the government distribute federally-owned surplus commodities to soup kitchens and other groups that provided free food to indigent people. This legislation was passed in response to growing reports of hunger among impoverished Americans (Congressional Quarterly Almanac 1983). A two-year extension of the surplus commodities distribution was passed later that year and was attached to PL 98-92 — an unemployment compensation bill. The unemployment rate in the U.S. peaked in 1982.

Reports and Documentation of Hunger (1983-1985)

In early 1983 members of Congress introduced several resolutions expressing their concern that food assistance programs should be protected from any further budget reductions. These resolutions were made in light of growing reports of hunger in America (USHR 1985a). The requirement that Puerto Rico furnish noncash benefits under its block grant was postponed until 1985. Also, in 1983, the Administration's Food Stamp budget proposals were rejected. On August 2, 1983, the United States Bureau of Labor Statistics reported that the Nation's poverty level was at its highest level since 1965. This report coupled with media reports of increased hunger spurred President Reagan to order a study of hunger in America (Congressional Quarterly Almanac 1983). The President's Task Force on Food Assistance was directed to measure the severity of the hunger problem and, if hunger was a serious problem, to recommend appropriate ways to address the issue (Brown 1989).

President's Task Force on Food Assistance. In its report issued January 9, 1984 the President's Task Force declared that rampant hunger could not be documented. Members of the President's Task Force, however, did not deny the existence of hunger in some segments of the U.S. population. Hunger, they concluded, was not a widespread national health problem. The report drew fire from anti-hunger advocates because the President's Task Force proposed that responsibility for food assistance should be that of the individual states. In addition, members of this task force recommended that harsher penalties be imposed against states not lowering their food stamp error rates. The President's Task Force, however, also recommended increasing the allowable assets to food stamp recipients and improving the collection of nutrition data (President's Task Force on Hunger in America 1984).

In 1984, the U.S. House of Representatives addressed the growing reports of hunger by establishing a Select Committee on Hunger. A similar committee operated in the Senate during the 1970s and was disbanded in 1977. The Committee addressed the issue of hunger in the U.S. and, also, the famine in Ethiopia. Congress crafted legislation which was designed to partially restore funding to food assistance programs (Congressional Quarterly Almanac 1984). Congress adjourned prior to completing action on these bills. In 1984 the House rejected HR 4684 a bill that would have coordinated a ten-year monitoring system of the nutritional status of Americans.

In 1985, Congress expanded food stamp eligibility and benefits. They did not complete action on a bill designed to expand child nutrition programs. In 1985 the Physician Task Force on Hunger in America concluded that hunger had reached epidemic proportions in the United States (Physician Task Force 1985).

Physician Task Force on Hunger in America. The Physician Task Force cited three pieces of evidence that hunger had increased. First, there was an increase in the number of households with incomes just above the poverty line (i.e., near-poor). In 1982, the Census Bureau estimated the number of people in poverty and the number of near poor to be 46.5 million people. By definition, incomes below the poverty level are too low to provide for minimally adequate diets. Increased poverty, according to the Physician Task Force, can result in increased hunger.

The second piece of evidence cited by the Physician Task Force, was the large number of hunger studies conducted in the United States in the 1980s. Investigators conducting studies across the U.S. all concluded that requests for food assistance grew at a tremendous rate during the first half of the decade. Many private food assistance groups reported an inability to keep pace with this increased demand for food (FRAC 1984).

The third piece of evidence cited by the Physician Task Force was an increase in health problems that are associated with hunger and malnutrition. Clinical manifestations of hunger appear more rapidly in malnourished children than in malnourished adults (Physician Task Force 1985). In early 1982, physicians at Boston Children's Hospital reported a substantial increase in the number of malnourished children examined. As a result of this report, the Massachusetts State Legislature appropriated funds for a year-long survey of 1,429 low income children (under the age of 6). According to the conductors of this survey, ten percent of the children in the study were suffering from chronic malnutrition and three percent of the children in the study were acutely malnourished. Twelve percent of these low income children were suffering from iron-deficiency anemia (Massachusetts Department of Public Health 1983).

Height, weight, and other body dimensions are frequently measured in well-infant and well-child medical examinations. This information is collected in order to establish baseline data of accepted norms for the population of the United States. The fifth percentile is the national norm below which one would only expect to find five percent of the children of a given age group. Several researchers indicated that more than five percent of poor children of all racial groups fell below this line (Physician Task Force 1985). Each year, the Centers for Disease Control [CDC] collects anthropometric data on low income children from 32 states. In 1982, 6–16 percent of children from birth to four years fell below the fifth percentile. These percentages were dependent upon ethnic groups. The groups at highest risk were Hispanic and American Indian four-year-olds (Brown and Allen 1988). The Massachusetts Nutrition Survey found growth deficits to be highly correlated with poverty. Furthermore, as family income increased, child growth patterns approached national norms (Massachusetts Department of Public Health 1983).

Frank, Allen, and Brown (1985) reported an increase in failure to thrive (FTT) among children who were being treated in low income clinics. This increase was among children whose families had recently lost benefits from one or more federal programs. Physicians concluded that lack of food was the critical problem for these children. Brams and Coury (1985) reported that good food supplementation programs decrease FTT risk. At Cook County Hospital in Chicago, physicians documented a 24% increase in admissions for FTT between 1981 and 1983. They also documented increased admissions for diarrhea and dehydration. Both of these conditions are serious nutrition-related diseases of children (Brown and Allen 1988).

The Infant Mortality Rate (IMR) is used as an indicator of health of the general population. IMR is based on the number of infants (per 1,000 live births) who die during the first year of life. In 1982, the U.S. rate was 11.2 and ranked eighteenth in the world. Most of western Europe, Japan, and Australia all ranked ahead of the U.S. (Physician Task Force 1985). Most of the infant mortality in the United States is believed to be due to premature and/or low birth weight infants (Physician Task Force 1985). The Surgeon General's Report: "Healthy People" (USDHHS 1979) set the goal of lowering the number of low birth weight babies to nine percent by 1990. The same report also listed poor maternal nutrition as a major cause of low birth weight infants.

Efforts to Alleviate the Hunger Problem (1986-1989)

Appropriations for senior nutrition programs were increased in 1986. Legislation to continue child nutrition programs was also passed. In 1987 Congress passed legislation (P.L. 100-77) designed to alleviate the problems of homeless Americans. This legislation included food assistance for the homeless. Also in this year, Congress ordered a pilot project in which the USDA would distribute surplus meat, poultry, fish, fruits, and vegetables to food banks. Cheese, butter, nonfat dry milk, cornmeal, flour, and rice would continue to be dispensed as before. In Public Law 100-232, Congress provided that eligibility for food stamps (by needy individuals) would not be affected by small cash contributions from private charities.

The National Nutrition Monitoring and Related Research Act of 1987 was passed by both houses of Congress. The bill, which would have provided for ongoing surveillance of the nutrition of Americans was pocket vetoed by Ronald Reagan in early 1988. Also in this year, a bill that would have provided for WIC participants to receive coupons redeemable at local farmers' markets was passed by the House. The bill was never acted upon by the Senate.

The Child Nutrition and WIC Reauthorization Act of 1989 (P.L. 101-147) provided for reauthorization of programs under the National School Lunch Act and the Child Nutrition Act. The law provided for permanent authorization of the School Lunch Program. Periodic renewals for WIC,

Summer Food Program and the Commodity Distribution Program would be required.

Summary

The government of the United States did not begin official measures to combat hunger among its population members until the 1930s. Prior to this, the task of feeding those unable to secure adequate food was assigned to churches, individuals, and philanthropic organizations. The economic depression of the 1930s marked a change in the way the U.S. dealt with hunger in its population.

The first food assistance program, the Food Stamp Plan, was developed as a combined measure to aid farmers and to help hungry people. The Food Stamp Plan was terminated when surplus commodities were needed to feed soldiers during World War II. Congress responded to the large number of draftees who were rejected, due to physical problems that had arisen because of childhood malnutrition, by inaugurating the School Lunch Program. The next time that hunger became an issue of national prominence occurred in the 1960 presidential campaign. After his election, Kennedy kept his campaign promise and reinstated the Food Stamp Plan. The Food Stamp Program became a fully funded government program in 1964. In 1966, the School Breakfast Program began.

In the late 1960s evidence of the existence of hunger in the United States began to emerge. As a result of this, data about the problem was collected by a variety of government and private groups. In the early 1970s, legislation designed to eradicate the problem was signed into law. WIC, "Meals on Wheels," and Congregate Meal programs for the elderly were all inaugurated at this time. From 1970 to 1977 existing food assistance programs were improved and expanded. In 1977, groups that had measured the extent of hunger in the late 1960s, declared that hunger was virtually eradicated in the U.S.

During the recession of the early 1980s, large budget reductions were made in the existing food assistance programs. Almost immediately, there were increased reports of people seeking assistance from food banks and food pantries. The President's Task Force on Hunger in America found no evidence of widespread hunger in the United States. Other groups studying the problem reported the existence of widespread hunger. One group, The Physician Task Force on Hunger in America, reported the existence of signs that hunger was returning to the U.S. and that 20 million Americans were experiencing hunger. At the end of the decade, despite lack of agreement as to the nature and extent of the problem, Congress voted to partially reinstate some of the funds that had been removed from food assistance programs at the beginning of the decade.

HUNGER SURVEYS AND THE NATIONAL NUTRITION MONITORING SYSTEM

Accurate data that has been collected in a reliable fashion is a critical cog in the policy formulation process, because it determines the theoretical needs of a given population (Hanft 1981). The importance of an accurate database has been championed by a number of health researchers. In Neustadt's (1978) analysis of the swine flu vaccination program, the author revealed how an inaccurate preliminary database assessment contributed to a misguided policy decision. Marmor (1970), writing about Medicare, explained how inaccurate preliminary estimates led to the adoption of policies that cost the Federal government millions of dollars. Collection of inaccurate data or inappropriate data can have serious ramifications for the policy formation process.

The first and crucial step in studying any health policy issue is establishing accurate and appropriate data with regard to the size and characteristics of the population (Bazzoli 1985). Backinger, Corbin, and Furman (1988) stated that the determination of incidence and prevalence is an important step in eradicating any public health problem. Terris (1986) emphasized the importance of knowing the population group and the characteristics (such as age, gender/sex, ethnic groups, occupation) of individuals afflicted with the health problem under investigation. Furthermore, according to Backinger, Corbin, and Furman (1988) the elimination of any public health problem cannot occur without the collection of baseline data, measurement of the problem at critical points, and the ability to measure directional changes in the problem. One way to achieve knowledge about the afflicted population group is through monitoring and surveillance of the problem.

At the present time, neither the government nor any private agency has a system in place for the continuous monitoring of hunger problems. Despite a large number of studies designed to measure the incidence and prevalence of hunger, there is still considerable debate as to its existence in the United States. While policy makers recognize that a hunger problem may exist, they doubt the validity of the hunger studies that have been conducted (Connecticut Association for Human Services 1986; Nestle and Guttmacher 1989). Policy makers addressing the problem of hunger in America must rely almost entirely on anecdotal information reported at Congressional committee hearings and on a hodgepodge of data collected by a variety of state, federal, and private agencies. Since the 1940s, when a large percentage of draftees were found unfit for service, the government has been engaged in periodic discussions of the need for nutrition surveillance of the U.S. population (Brown 1984).

Measurement of Nutritional Status by the Government

Currently, surveillance and monitoring of nutritional status and available nutrients is conducted by several agencies of the federal government. The two main agencies involved in monitoring the nutritional status of Americans are the Department of Health and Human Services [USDHHS] and the United States Department of Agriculture [USDA]. In the Food and Agriculture Act of 1977, Congress asked that a plan for nutrition monitoring be submitted. The plan would provide for integration and coordination of surveys conducted by the Department of Health and Human Services, the United States Department of Agriculture, and all government agencies involved in the measurement of food composition, food supply, food consumption, health and nutrition status, dietary knowledge, and attitude assessment.

After refinements by the Government Accounting Office [GAO], this plan for a nutrition monitoring system was submitted to the Congress in 1981. The Joint Implementation Plan for a Comprehensive National Nutrition Monitoring System had two main objectives. The first objective called for appropriate coordination between the two largest surveys conducted — National Health and Nutrition Examination Survey or NHANES (conducted by USDHHS) and National Food Consumption Survey or NFCS (conducted by USDA). The second objective called for the development of a reporting system that would integrate information from NHANES, NFCS, and other monitoring efforts. Information regarding the nutritional status of Americans would then be reported to

Congress. This system of reporting would ensure that the government would speak with one voice when setting nutrition policy for the Nation.

Until recently, The Joint Implementation Plan for a Comprehensive National Nutrition Monitoring System was never mandated by law. Beginning in 1981, a series of bills that would provide for the National Nutrition Monitoring System [NNMS] to be governed by law, were introduced in both houses of Congress. The National Nutrition Monitoring and Related Research Act of 1987 cleared both houses of Congress on October 18, 1987. After this approval, however, the legislation was pocket vetoed by President Reagan on November 8. President Reagan stated that the bill would provide for excessive bureaucracy and expense (Congressional Quarterly Almanac 1988). On October 22, 1990, the National Nutrition Monitoring and Related Research Act was signed into law. The law established, among other things, a ten-year national nutrition monitoring research program and a national nutrition monitoring research council. Public Law 101-445 also mandated that low income groups be continually monitored for adequate dietary intakes. It did not, however, describe how this monitoring is to be accomplished.

Prior to the passage of this law, a National Nutrition Monitoring System had existed in the United States. The duties of this system included establishing baseline data, collecting, analyzing, and disseminating nutritional and dietary data regarding the citizenry of the U.S. High-risk groups and nutrition-related problems and trends were to be identified so that appropriate intervention strategies could be initiated (USDHHS and USDA 1986). These objectives were to be accomplished using five assessment techniques. These data collection methods included: 1) nutritional and health status measurements; 2) food composition measurements; 3) food consumption measurements; 4) assessments of dietary knowledge and attitudes; and 5) food supply determinations.

The U.S. Department of Health and Human Services (1989) has made suggestions for improving the National Nutrition Monitoring System. First, in order to achieve a comprehensive system of monitoring and surveillance, the NNMS components must be fully coordinated. Second, the research base for nutrition monitoring should be improved. Surveillance data collected by researchers outside of the federal government should be used as well as information regarding survey techniques. Third, timely reporting and immediate interpretation of the data also play a role of critical importance in surveillance techniques. Last, the information exchange between policy makers and researchers should be enhanced.

In *Nutrition Monitoring in the United States* (USDHHS 1989), it was noted that poverty may result in hunger or the inability to maintain good nutritional status. Additionally, the authors suggested that improvements should be made to nutritional monitoring of at-risk populations (USDHHS 1989). According to the authors of this report, a paucity of data from NNMS makes it impossible to accurately assess the occurrence and impact of hunger (USDHHS 1989).

Hunger Studies in the 1980s

A lack of timely monitoring and surveillance by NNMS resulted in a situation in which reports of hunger were increasing (in the media) at a time when the government lacked information regarding the incidence and prevalence of the problem. Recognition of the need to accurately measure and record the problem, resulted in the employment of a variety of methods to study hunger in the United States. These methods were employed by federal agencies, state agencies, and private organizations in an attempt to fill this information void.

The federal government itself pursued several avenues of exploration of the hunger problem. Congress heard testimony from hungry individuals, soup kitchen and food bank proprietors, and anti-hunger advocates (FRAC 1984). A 1983 study conducted by the Government Accounting Office concluded that the number of individuals seeking emergency food assistance had increased. The most notable government attempt to document the existence and prevalence of a widespread undernutrition problem was the President's Task Force on Food Assistance (1984). This report, based on hearings conducted in cities across the U.S., concluded that widespread hunger did not exist.

Most efforts to measure hunger in the 1980s did not come from the federal government, but from the private sector. This is an interesting departure from other public health problems. One group that embarked upon an effort to document the hunger problem was the United States Conference of Mayors. In October of 1982, this bipartisan group released a study that reported a significant increase in the number of individuals seeking emergency food in cities across the country. Mayor Coleman Young of Detroit cited an almost fivefold increase in the number of households being served by emergency food assistance programs between 1980 and 1982 (FRAC 1984). In a companion report issued in June of

1983, the U.S. Conference of Mayors reported that most of the emergency food assistance programs operating in their cities had been established within the previous three years (Physician Task Force 1985). Each year since 1982, the U.S. Conference of Mayors has issued a report regarding the hunger situation in selected American cities. The authors of each report concluded that there is a need for emergency food assistance in most American cities.

National reports have also been conducted by various religious groups. Traditionally, in times of need, Americans have turned to the churches for food assistance. In 1982 the National Council of Churches found hunger to be three and even four times worse in some regions of the country. The National Conference of Catholic Charities reported that they provided twice the amount of emergency meals in 1982 as in 1981. The United Church of Christ reported in January of 1983 a 40–200 percent increase in the number of people seeking help from their emergency food centers in the period of time reviewed. "Hunger Watch U.S.A." coordinated by Bread for The World, a Christian organization, attempted to document increases in the number of food requests. The Hunger Watches conducted throughout the U.S. at various sites and at various times, consistently corroborated all other studies. There was a significantly great demand being placed on the private food assistance programs in the U.S. (FRAC 1984).

In addition to the government agencies and church affiliates, two notable national studies were conducted by two anti-hunger advocacy groups. The Food Research and Action Council conducted a survey of individuals using emergency food centers in 14 states. In its 1983 report, FRAC found that two-thirds of the clientele were recipients of food stamps. Of this group, three-fourths reported that their food stamps lasted two to three weeks of the month. FRAC also published a guide designed to aid communities in documenting hunger and began collecting studies from across the country in order to build an extensive file of hunger studies.

The second notable study, was that conducted by the Physician Task Force on Hunger in America. The Physician Task Force (1985) issued a report based on a similar study conducted by the Citizens' Board of Inquiry in the late 1960s. Their study of hunger counties concluded that 20 million Americans experienced hunger and that 40 million were in danger of hunger. The federal government countered by issuing a rebuttal to this study (GAO 1986). A Harris poll conducted in the same time period asked Americans if they knew of anyone experiencing hunger. The pollsters concluded that roughly 21 million Americans experienced hunger (Harris 1984).

In addition to these national studies, dozens of state and local studies concluded that there was a tremendous increase in the number of Americans requesting food assistance during the decade of the 1980s. None of the authors of these studies reported either a reduction or a stabilization of requests for food assistance. All investigators reported documented increases in the number of people requesting food assistance (FRAC 1984; Physician Task Force 1985).

Although many studies were conducted during the decade, little effort has been made to integrate the results of the studies. The Physician Task Force (1985) discussed some of the major studies conducted. This discussion, however, was primarily a narrative review. The Food Research and Action Center discussed some of the results of selected studies in their 1984 publication. Brown (1989), listed (to the best of his knowledge) all hunger studies performed to date. Nestle and Guttmacher (1989) integrated results from selected state hunger studies which were obtained from the FRAC files. In fact, many hunger studies and reports discuss, in narrative form, the conclusions reached by other investigators. Little attempt was made, until this book, to integrate numerical information collected by the various studies.

Types of Hunger Studies

During the 1980s, research designed to investigate the hunger problem consisted of three basic study types: anecdotal, report, and survey. In the anecdotal study little attempt was made to quantify the data. Instead, short vignettes or stories about specific households were recorded and reported. Participants were asked to give a verbal portrait of their households. This type of study was the least scientific and most difficult to analyze. In some instances the researchers culled information from these interviews and reported specific information in a numerical format.

In the report study type, relevant information about hunger and associated determinants was discussed. Generally, these reports used existing data such as census tract data, unemployment figures, and poverty figures to formulate estimates of the number of hungry people within the sample parameters. The report method was used to create a profile of at-risk groups in a given community. Researchers did not obtain information from users or providers, but, rather, used statistical information that could be drawn from state, local, and national data. In other instances, the data could not be provided and was estimated by the researchers. This resulted in researchers estimating the number of individuals in a given locale who were, for example, not receiving food stamps. It should be noted that this type of study was very often performed by states and municipal governments and was more commonly conducted at the beginning of the decade.

The third type of hunger study was the survey method. Surveys were conducted by phone, by mail, administered orally by an interviewer, or completed in writing by the respondent. Respondents were asked questions that dealt with basic demographic characteristics such as gender and age. In some studies, the respondents were asked whether or not they were experiencing hunger.

Hunger investigators studied a diversity of population groups including users of food pantries, soup kitchens, surplus commodity distribution sites, social service agencies, and emergency assistance sites. Members of general population samples and low income population samples were also selected for study. Clients, providers, elected officials, citizens, and selected citizens (e.g., low income citizens) all appeared in some type of hunger investigation. Hunger researchers also selected and studied urban, rural, and suburban settings.

The method of reporting was almost as varied as the type of hunger study. Some investigators employed a strictly scientific method of reporting in which methods, subjects and procedures, were clearly delineated in the report. Others, reported their findings in the form of anecdotal or a kind of narrative storytelling of these studies. Thus, it was sometimes difficult to ascertain the results of the study.

Summary

Establishing an accurate database is a vital component of the policy formulation process. One way in which to establish such a database is through monitoring and surveillance of the population at-risk. Yet, at the present time, there is no system in place for the continuous monitoring of the population groups who are at risk for hunger. Since there is no overall method of reporting hunger, policy makers in the U.S. have been forced to rely on information from a variety of hunger studies conducted by an assortment of groups and individuals.

In the 1980s when the issue of hunger became the subject of political debate, hundreds of studies were conducted in an effort to document hunger. At the national level, the government produced several notable studies including that of the President's Task Force on Hunger in America. This task force concluded that hunger in epidemic proportions did not exist in the United States. Two noteworthy national studies conducted by independent groups (The Physician Task Force and FRAC) concluded that hunger did, indeed, exist in epidemic proportions. The U.S. Conference of Mayors reported yearly, throughout the decade, that hunger was growing in the U.S. A host of churches, states, food assistance agencies, and municipalities arrived at a variety of conclusions regarding the nature and extent of the problem. Studies conducted during this period can be broken into three basic methodological types — report, survey, and anecdotal. The survey method is the study type that will be examined in the quantitative portion of this study.

III

Method and Procedure

Some of the purposes of this study were to construct a profile of individuals who sought emergency food assistance at soup kitchens and food banks, to examine to what extent these characteristics were associated with perceived hunger, to assess and review survey methodology employed in the measurement of hunger statistics, and to investigate the use of meta-analysis for studying surveys. An overview of meta-analytic methodology precedes a discussion of the subject identification, subject selection, and the development of the two systems used in this survey. The first system, The Descriptors for Coded Categorical Variables, was designed to normalize variables for seventeen hunger categories. The second system, The Survey Weighting System, was developed to give studies of a higher methodological and administrative caliber greater numerical impact.

OVERVIEW OF META-ANALYSIS

The term meta-analysis was coined by Glass (1976) and refers to a quantitative approach to reviewing large numbers of related research studies. In the traditional narrative review, the author discusses studies that address a specific research problem. To compensate for the lack of a quantitative component in the traditional narrative review, investigators have adopted a variety of quantitative tools including box scores, rank-ordering, and vote-counts (Kite and Johnson 1988; Fernandez and Turk

1989; Hall and Dornan 1990; Jones 1995). Meta-analysis is a research tool that was developed in order to add more objectivity to the review process through the use of sophisticated statistics (Fernandez and Turk 1989; Dickersin and Berlin 1992).

Until recently, meta-analysis was largely confined to aggregating knowledge in the social sciences — particularly in the field of psychology (Dickersin and Berlin 1992; Jones 1995). In their review of health journals, Louis, Fineberg, and Mosteller (1985) discovered an increase in the number of studies employing meta-analytic techniques. Goodman (1989) has reported that meta-analysis has become the subject of increased attention in the medical literature. In 1989 "meta-analysis" was adapted by MEDLINE as a subject heading and in 1993 MEDLINE adopted "meta-analysis" as publication type (Dickersin and Berlin 1992). Louis, Fineberg, Mosteller (1985) concluded that meta-analysis is receiving increased attention in public health primarily because meta-analysis yields stronger conclusions than other types of comparative studies.

According to some researchers there are two types of meta-analysis: primary and secondary (Bangert-Drowns 1986). In primary meta-analysis the original data from each study are obtained and analyzed. In secondary meta-analysis the conclusive data (e.g., correlative data) are analyzed using various statistical techniques. Some researchers have proposed that primary meta-analysis is the far more powerful analytic technique because it employs the original sample data (Hultsman and Black 1989; Bailar 1995). Other proponents of meta-analysis argue that there is no such thing as primary meta-analysis (Glass and Kliegl 1983). Glass and Kliegl (1983) maintain that meta-analysis is, by its very definition, an analysis of summary statistics from related studies. Original data is often difficult if not impossible to obtain. Many good studies, therefore, would be eliminated because of the fact that the original data is unobtainable. Secondary analysis is a far more useable research tool because of the accessibility of the data.

Steps of the Meta-Analysis Process

Although most authors discuss meta-analysis in terms of a four-step process, Cordray (1990) and Jenicek (1989) argue for the inclusion of an additional two steps to the meta-analytic framework. These two additional steps which are integral in the research process include: 1) clear specification of the research question (s) for examination and 2) clear delineation of the research domain under consideration. A typical meta-analysis, then, can be discussed in terms of six steps:

1) specification of the research question(s)
2) delineation of the research domain
3) review of the literature;
4) assessment of the literature;
5) analysis of the sample; and
6) summary of the analysis.

Specification of the research question(s). Specification of a research question is of primary importance in any investigation. Research reviews, in general, are frequently vague with regard to the principal question of the study (Light and Pillemer 1984). In the case of a meta-analytic review, failure to clarify the question will result in the formation of barriers to a successful study (Rothstein and McDaniel 1989). Without clear definition of the research question(s), it is impossible to set the appropriate parameters for the research domain (Cordray 1990; Hasselblad et al. 1995).

Delineation of the research domain. After specification of the research question(s), the boundaries of the research domain must be determined. This step is also referred to as delineating the population for the study (Cordray 1990). In a meta-analysis, the population from which the subjects will be drawn refers to studies. The choices of the domain (or population) will have far-reaching ramifications with regard to generalizing the results (Cordray 1990).

The research domain should be specified in terms of whether or not the reviewer will search domestic or international journals and what parameters the researcher will set for study inclusion. When setting this domain, the researcher must always keep in mind the research question (Light and Pillemer 1984; Rothstein and McDaniel 1989).

Choosing an appropriate time frame is also crucial to domain specification. This is often neglected by the meta-analyst (Meinert 1989). The researcher should also consider the time frame in terms of the research question.

Review of the literature. Review of the literature might be better termed retrieval of the literature (Strube and Hartmann 1983). The researcher systematically reviews reliable databases in order to discover studies that are relevant to the study question. Criteria for judging inclusion of a study in the review of literature must be established prior to the database searches (Bailar 1995). Establishing the research domain prior to the database searches will aid in delineating the key words and the appropriate databases. Besides databases, reference lists and review articles should be scanned. Scanning back issues of selected journals may also produce relevant studies (Hultsman and Black 1989).

The review of literature is an element of meta-analysis that is subject to several problems. First, all appropriate databases must be searched. Chalmers (1990) cites "slothful" literature reviews as the reason for unsuccessful reviews. The "key words" used for each database search must be chosen with care. Rothstein and McDaniel (1989) contend that computerized searches must be supplemented with manual searches. Failure in this section of the meta-analysis may cause inadvertent exclusion of relevant studies. Too narrow a literature search, then, introduces a sampling bias (Dickersin and Berlin 1992). The validity of a meta-analysis, then, is dependent upon the thoroughness of the literature search (McCartney, Harris, and Bernieri 1990).

Second, the question of whether or not unpublished data sources should be included is a controversial one. Some investigators do not include unpublished sources such as dissertations because of a belief that if the research is well-done it would have been published (Slavin 1995). They also cite difficulty in obtaining unpublished sources as another reason for lack of inclusion in the meta-analysis. Unpublished data sources are sometimes difficult to find (e.g., reports of various agencies).

Many meta-analysts, however, stress the inclusion of both published and unpublished studies in the defined content domain (Bullock and Svyantek 1985; Chalmers 1990; Slavin 1995). Due to the fact that journal editors may choose studies that are statistically significant or confirm previously published reports, good studies not meeting with editorial policies may remain unpublished (Dickersin 1990). Dickersin and Berlin (1992) concluded that, since publication bias occurs, unpublished studies should not be discounted as scientifically irrelevant. These researchers indicated that publication bias is a great problem (Dickersin and Berlin 1992). Wolf (1986) noted that, because many studies with negative results are never published, it is necessary to compute fail-safe N. This computation results in the number of additional studies that would be necessary to reverse a conclusion that was based on both published and unpublished data (Wolf 1986).

Assessment of the literature. After obtaining all relevant studies the reviewer must decide which studies will be included in the data analysis section. Deciding on criteria for selection is, indeed, a highly subjective process (Wortman 1983). The researcher must decide upon a system of choosing studies and establish criteria for selection early on in the study. The criteria should be applied to each study discovered in the review of literature. Much controversy surrounds the issue of inclusion criterion.

Some researchers argue that all studies must be included, irrespective of study design (Strube and Hartmann 1983). The assumption being made by these researchers is that the analysis will ascertain where biases exist. One method of deciding which studies to include is by adopting a system of coding study quality (Dickersin and Berlin 1992). This serves two purposes. First it provides a quantitative method of reviewing studies for inclusion in the meta-analysis. Second, it can point out potential procedural or design problems of studies, thus aiding future research (Strube and Hartmann 1983).

The inclusion of inappropriate studies may produce inappropriate conclusions. This is a particular problem when a small number of studies are used (Bullock and Svyantek 1985). In small samples, a single study can skew the data. Researchers can use large samples of studies and include only appropriate studies (Bullock and Svyantek 1985). Alternatively, investigators can compensate for the effects of small, but well-designed studies through the use of weighting.

One way to establish a method for the selection of appropriate studies is by examining studies for validity. Strube and Hartmann (1982) outline three types of validity that should be examined when assessing data quality. Conceptual validity refers to whether or not a study tests what it purports to test. Researchers may report that they tested a specific question when they did not, or conversely, researchers may test a specific question when they did not report testing of the question (Light and Pillemer 1984). Methodological validity is a determination of the quality of the hypothesis test. Statistical validity determines whether or not appropriate statistical techniques were employed in testing the hypothesis.

Researchers also use a variety of rating systems in order to give greater weight to better studies. This allows the investigator to use all studies, but to rate the better studies higher on the scale. It is important that a list of studies used in the analysis, the codification scheme be made public in the meta-analysis report (Bullock and Svyantek 1985). Clear discussion of inclusion and exclusion criteria is a necessity if studies are to be replicable (O'Rourke and Detsky 1989). This discussion will aid future investigative efforts.

Analysis of the sample. After careful selection of appropriate studies, standard statistical techniques are used to interpret the data. Analysis of the data can be done by any of a wide variety of statistical techniques. Care must be taken to use appropriate statistical techniques for the data collected. Results of meta-analysis can vary depending on what statistical technique is employed (Strube and Hartmann 1983).

In the past, analysis of summary statistics could be divided into two categories: assessing the effect size and assessing the significance levels (Strube and Hartmann 1983). Summarizing of results across studies using a combination of effect sizes is an approach advocated by Glass (1976). There are a great number of methods that can be employed for estimating effect size (Jones 1995). The effect size approach, however, is most effective for use in applied areas where a treatment effect has been observed (Strube and Hartmann 1982).

In studies where an effect size was not measured, meta-analysts must use other statistics to analyze the data. This area of meta-analysis is beginning to grow, as evidenced by recent studies which have analyzed data from research that did not involve a specific measurable treatment effect. Meta-analysts must choose statistics appropriate to the data collected from the studies. Cordray (1990) has recommended development of meta-analytic statistical methods that can be used with survey research.

Summary of the analysis. One of the crucial procedures in the meta-analysis process is the summary step. In this step information is coalesced and the research questions are answered. Frequently, this section of the meta-analysis is afforded abbreviated thought and space.

Procedurally, this section does not have the same controversies associated with it as do the preceding steps. In this section, the meta-analyst is charged with two duties. First, the hypothesis question must be answered based on information gathered in the study. Second, the researcher should formulate new hypotheses and research questions based on the results of the study. These duties are not unique to meta-analysis, but are characteristics of summary sections of all studies. Because of the detailed analysis of study design, the meta-analyst has a great deal of information regarding the characteristics of good study design for future studies in the area of interest (Dickersin and Berlin 1992; Fiske 1983).

Meta-Analysis and Policy Planning

After the summary of the analysis, the meta-analyst is in a unique position for policy planning. Bangert-Drowns (1986) suggests that valuable information is scattered across the literature and meta-analysis is the technique that can bring this information together. The resulting information can be used by social scientists to answer basic policy questions (Bangert-Drowns 1986). Jenicek (1989) states that well-organized studies using the meta-analytic technique provide important information for policy makers. Policy makers need the best possible evaluation of current data in order to set appropriate health policies and programs.

Policy analysts who use meta-analysis are also in a position to discover trends. Based on the extensive examination of available research, the meta-analyst should recognize and discuss general trends related to the question of interest. This examination of trends is of particular interest to policy analysts.

Meta-analysis, then, would seem to lend itself to the discipline of policy analysis for two reasons. First, policy analysts use existing data and, through secondary analyses, glean useable data. This reduces the need to generate new data and, therefore, saves time and money (Dickersin and Berlin 1992). Second, there is a need for policy makers to participate in the design of information collection systems (Solomon and Shortell 1981). In fact, a policy analyst should know how to merge data sets and aggregate data from multiple sources in order to examine broad policy issues. Linking data sets from multiple sources prove a useful tool to a policy analyst.

Strengths and Weaknesses of Meta-Analysis

Meta-analysis, however, is not without its critics. It has both strengths and weaknesses, as does any research methodology (McCartney, Harris, and Bernieri 1990; Jones 1995; Liberati 1995). Some of these strengths have been discussed in the preceding paragraphs. An examination of the strengths and weaknesses of meta-analysis is provided in the following paragraphs.

A major criticism of the narrative review is the high degree of subjectivity in the process (Fernandez and Turk 1989). Meta-analysis minimizes the subjective nature of the narrative review. The selection of the time frame, the research domain, the research question and the literature review all can introduce subjectivity and bias. Indeed, the statistical analysis, the very thing that was to add objectivity, may be subjective. The statistics selected to study the data may actually present the data in a biased fashion. The systematization of the process makes the entire meta-analytic study a matter of public record, however, and subjective matters can be readily examined by the reader (Fiske 1983; Powe et al. 1994).

According to Hall and Dornan (1990), it is the use of quantitative statistics that places the meta-analyst in a unique position to discover less obvious trends than the narrative reviewer. Small trends or trends that are inconsistent in one direction are more likely to be discovered by the meta-analyst than the narrative reviewer. Results from poorly designed studies, however, may skew results (Nagasawa et al. 1990) and does not mend data from poor studies.

Poorly designed studies have the power to cause a skew in the quantified results. It is, therefore, prudent to devise some method of assessing the validity of the study. Questions of validity are of profound importance in the meta-analytic review.

Hall and Dornan (1990) concluded that the systematic nature of the meta-analysis makes it possible for the meta-analyst to review a large number of studies. A narrative reviewer might be overwhelmed by the numbers of studies, but the meta-analytic reviewer's use of statistics makes the review of large numbers of studies possible (Hall and Dornan 1990).

Summary

The research technique of meta-analysis has recently gained favor as a method for studying health issues. This procedure has been embraced by many investigators in the health field because of its ability to aid in the review of results of large numbers of studies. Unlike its cousin, the narrative review, results from a large number of studies can be combined with the use of statistics. The meta-analytic process consists of the following six steps: specification of the research questions(s); delineation of the research domain; review of the literature; assessment of the literature; analysis of the sample; and summary of the analysis.

There are several important considerations that impact heavily on the success of a meta-analysis. Obtaining all the research studies in the domain of study is critical to a successful meta-analysis. The guidelines for the determination of study selection must be decided upon early in the investigation and then must be uniformly applied to all studies. After selection of the studies that will be used, the quantitative statistical analysis can be performed. Using statistics that are appropriate to the data collected from the studies is imperative to a successful outcome. Finally in the summary step, the information is coalesced and the research questions are answered. This final step calls for careful observation of the results.

Critics find that meta-analyses have many of the same problems of narrative reviews. Subjectivity can be introduced in the selection of the time frame, the research domain, the research questions, and the statistical analysis. In addition to these problems, the inherent problems and limitations of each individual study can cause problems in the meta-analysis. Poor studies may produce bad statistics. Proponents of meta-analysis, however, state that this problem can be counteracted by weighting studies with regard to the quality of study design. The systematic nature of the meta-analysis, proponents claim, means that all objectivity in the design and conduct of the research is a matter of public record. Meta-analysis may be a useful tool to policy analysts because its systematic review makes review of a large number of studies possible and this makes the discovery of small, less obvious trends possible.

STUDY IDENTIFICATION

Several authors (Bullock and Svyantek 1985; Slavin 1995) emphasize the importance of including published and unpublished studies in the meta-analysis. A critical aim of this investigation, then, was to garner all hunger studies conducted during the established time frame of 1981–1989. This time frame was chosen because it encompasses the decade of the 1980's — a decade which began with increased reports of hunger in the United States. In order to accomplish this goal, a strategy for discovering studies was formulated. This system of locating hunger studies was comprised of three strategies for collecting studies.

Strategy One: Indices of Published Literature

Strategy one was employed in an effort to discover published hunger studies. After consultation with a reference librarian (at the University of Illinois at Urbana-Champaign), several databases were selected for review. *Cumulated Index Medicus* was searched in order to reveal hunger studies published in health and medical journals. A search of the *Social Science Citation Index* and the *Social Sciences Index* (on Wilsondisc) culled hunger studies published in social science journals. Hunger studies conducted as part of the fulfillment of Ph.D. requirements, were discovered in the *Dissertation Abstracts Index*. An inspection of *The Readers' Guide to Periodical Literature* resulted in a list of hunger surveys published in popular magazines. Similarly, the *Newspaper Citation Index* and *Newsbank* were examined in order to locate hunger studies published in the newspaper medium. Searching both newspaper guides was deemed essential to revealing hunger studies that may have found no other venue for publication than the popular press. The Public Affairs Information Service database was searched in order to disclose documents published by the U.S. government.

Strategy Two: Food Research and Action Center Files

The author spent a week at the offices of the Food Research and Action Center in Washington, DC during January of 1990. FRAC was established in 1970 as a nonpartisan, nonprofit organization comprised of nutritionists, lawyers, and activists who devote their efforts to alleviating hunger, malnutrition, and poverty in the United States. FRAC endeavors to strengthen federal food assistance programs by working in the areas of policy analysis, litigation, public information, research, and grassroots activities. FRAC maintains one of the most extensive files of hunger studies assembled in one location (Nestle and Guttmacher 1989). Lynn Parker, Director of Nutrition Policy and Research at FRAC invited the author to visit FRAC and make copies of all available hunger studies. This strategy was necessary in order to collect unpublished studies.

Strategy Three: Survey of State Health Departments, Hunger Agencies, and Hunger Activists

The final strategy was used in order to find studies, published or unpublished, that had not appeared in either Strategy One (the indexes of published literature) or Strategy Two (the FRAC files). In order to discover these surveys, letters of inquiry were sent to appropriate agencies and to leaders in hunger investigation in the U.S. The letters requested copies of hunger studies collected by the particular agency, state, or locale. Additionally, recipients of the letter were requested to supply information regarding any hunger studies of which they were aware.

Public health departments in each of the 50 states (and Washington, DC) were included, as well as individuals and specific agencies known to be involved in the hunger movement. While reviewing hunger surveys already obtained, the author discovered surveys mentioned in reports, but not included in the studies collected to that point. An attempt was made to obtain these studies. The addresses of the public health departments and individuals were obtained in the following manner:

1. State department of public health addresses were obtained from a list of government addresses listed in *State Administrative Officials Classified by Function 1989-1990* (1989).

2. A mailing list was developed for the purpose of contacting individuals (or agencies) who might know of existing hunger surveys. The list includes individuals who are active in U.S. hunger issues, agencies that have already conducted hunger studies, and agencies that might have been involved in a hunger study. The names of the agencies mentioned in the latter group were obtained in the author's extensive reading of hunger reports, hunger studies and media reports.

STUDY SELECTION

An exhaustive search for all existing published and unpublished hunger studies (1981-1989) resulted in a large pool of reports. A systematic analysis of these collected hunger studies was then undertaken. This search was consistent with Jenicek's (1989) proposal that the key ingredient in a successful meta-analysis is a continuity achieved by a methodical analysis of all available studies. The Flow Chart of Analysis (Figure One) is a modification of a flow chart introduced by Jenicek.

In Step One of the meta-analysis (see Figure One) each of the hunger studies was examined for its method of data collection. The type of study design employed by each individual survey was determined. Only those studies employing survey methodological techniques were of interest to this investigation.

In Step Two, studies that used survey methodology were identified according to survey type (mail, telephone, personal interview, questionnaire); respondent type (clients, providers, officials, low income people, other); survey site (soup kitchen, food pantry, government office, home, other); and method of reporting (anecdotal, numerical report, unusable numerical report). Surveys containing anecdotal summations or inappropriate numerical reporting were excluded at this time. Surveys that met all survey criteria, but lacked any type of hunger perception index, were used only to provide descriptive statistics in this investigation.

In Step Three, surveys were examined and weighted based on sample selection, survey design, use of a hunger perception measurement, and the method of reporting the results. Studies which were poorly designed, conducted and reported received lower total weighting scores. This weighting system was used to give statistical consideration to survey strength. Thus, better surveys merited higher scores.

The data analysis was conducted in Step Four. Descriptive statistics and Pearson product-moment correlation procedures were used to analyze the data. These statistics were computed using the data values after weighting. Additionally, scatterplots were examined for possible correlations.

INSTRUMENTATION

Two systems were developed for use in this investigation: The Descriptors for Coded Categorical Variables and The Survey Weighting System. Utilization of these two systems provided a framework for normalizing the responses and then weighting the value of the responses prior to data analysis.

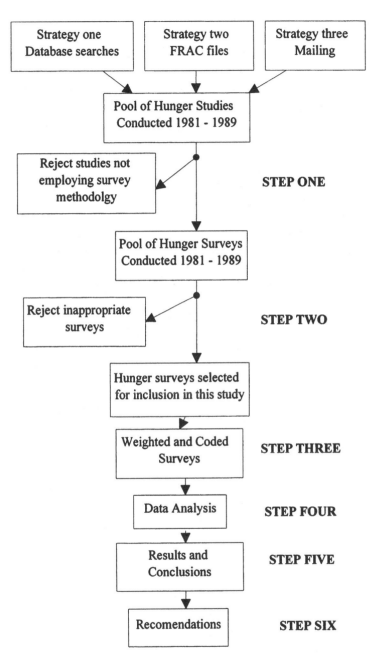

Figure 1. Flow Chart of Analysis. (After Jenicek, 1990)

Descriptors for Coded Categorical Variables

The Descriptors for Coded Categorical Variables was designed to delineate areas that consistently appear in hunger surveys and to provide a way in which the responses could be normalized. Once normalized and coded, data from different surveys was used to provide descriptive statistics and, in some instances, correlational data. This information was then used to answer some of the research questions.

The seventeen categories of central hunger questions were chosen in the following manner. All of the collected hunger studies were read and examined for the areas of questions asked of hungry individuals. Based on this, seventeen categories (or central hunger questions) were chosen. These subject areas (categories) were compared to several National studies (U.S. Conference of Mayors 1982, 1983a, 1983b, 1984, 1986a, 1986b, 1987a, 1987b, 1988, 1989; Physician Task Force 1985; Connecticut Association For Human Services 1986).

The surveys chosen for inclusion in this study were individually analyzed for each category of questions (e.g., participation in the Food Stamp Program). After repeated examination of each of the surveys, appropriate descriptors were determined. The seventeen categories and descriptors are depicted in Table 1.

Coding category one: Gender/Sex. This category was coded for three possible responses: male, female, and no response/missing data.

Coding category two: Ethnic group. Different surveys inquired about ethnicity in a variety of ways. Questions in the ethnic group category sought to determine whether or not respondents belonged to a minority group and, if so, what minority group. In order to accommodate all studies, data for all nonwhites was collapsed to produce one category that was then compared to the percent of whites. Then, values for four minority groups (American Indian, Asian, Black, Hispanic) and whites were compared. "Other", then, referred to minorities other than the ones used in this coding scheme. In some instances, other referred to any of the four minority groups used in this coding category.

Coding category three: Age. Codification of the age category presented difficulties because surveys asked age both as an absolute numerical value (How old are you?) and in terms of ranges. Since each

Table 1: Descriptors for Coded Categorical Variables

Coding Category	Descriptor
One: Gender/Sex	1. Male 2. Female
Two: Ethnic Group	1. White 2. Nonwhite 3. American Indian 4. Asian 5. Black 6. Hispanic 7. Other
Three: Age	1. Actual Mean 2. Artificial Mean
Four: Marital Status	1. Married 2. Unmarried 3. Cohabiting 4. Divorced/Separated 5. Single 6. Widowed
Five: Education	1. Less than High School Diploma 2. High School Diploma or GED 3. More than High School
Six: Employment Status	1. Employed 2. Unemployed 3. Full-time Job 4. Part-time Job 5. More than 1 Part-time Job 6. Temporary 7. Seasonal 8. Disabled 9. Retired
Seven: Income	1. At 100% of Poverty 2. At 125% of Poverty

Table 1: Descriptors for Coded Categorical Variables

Coding Category	Descriptor
Eight: Income Source	1. AFDC 2. Alimony 3. Child Support 4. Church 5. Disability/Worker's Compensation 6. Food Stamps 7. General Assistance 8. Gifts — Family and Friends 9. Home Relief 10. Pensions/Retirement 11. Salaries 12. Savings 13. Social Security Retirement Income 14. Social Security Disability Income 15. Supplemental Security Income 16. Title 19 17. Unemployment Compensation 18. Utility Assistance 19. Veterans' Benefits 20. Other 21. No Income
Nine: Household Size	1. One 2. Two 3. Three 4. Four 5. Five 6. Six and over
Ten: Household Composition	1. Single adult/no children 2. Single adult/with children 3. More than one adult/no children 4. More than one adult/children 5. Households with children 6. Average number of children per household 7. Average age of children 8. Households with elderly

Table 1: Descriptors for Coded Categorical Variables

Coding Category	Descriptor
Eleven: Special Dietary Needs	1. Do you (or a member of your household) require a special diet? 2. What type of special diet is required? 3. Have you (or a member of your family) been treated for a hunger-related illness? 4. Are you (or a member of your household) pregnant or lactating?
Twelve: Food Stamp Participation	1. Are you receiving food stamps? 2. How many months have you received food stamps? 3. Do your food stamps ever run out? 4. Have you received food stamps in the past? 5. If you are not currently receiving food stamps, what is the reason for not receiving?
Thirteen: Participation in Other Government Food Assistance Programs	1. Elderly Feeding Program 2. School Breakfast 3. School Lunch 4. WIC 5. Surplus Commodities
Fourteen: Participation in Government Assistance Programs	1. AFDC 2. Social Security 3. SSI 4. Veterans' Benefits 5. Medicare 6. Medicaid 7. Other

Table 1: Descriptors for Coded Categorical Variables

Coding Category	Descriptor
Fifteen: Hunger Participation	1. Percentage of individuls who say they are hungry 2. Percentage of households where meals are skipped. 3. Percentage of children without food
Sixteen: Living Conditions	1. Are you homeless? 2. Do you have access to cooking facilities? 3. Do you own, rent, or live with relatives/friends?
Seventeen: Geographic Location	1. Region of the U.S. 2. Urban 3. Rural 4. Suburban

study employed a different age range, it was necessary to take the midpoint of a range and determine an artificial mean. In cases where a true mean was available, this value was used. Ranges that sought to determine the number of children under eighteen and the number of senior citizens were included as variables in this category. This was done in order to maintain information about these two important age groups.

Coding category four: Marital status. Surveys examined marital status in many different ways. In its simplest form, marital status was coded as either married or unmarried. Some studies asked for a type of unmarried status (single, divorced, separated, widowed, or cohabiting). In order to give proper consideration to all studies, marital status was coded and measured in the following way. Specific information regarding the status of unmarried individuals was coded as separate descriptors (cohabiting, divorced/separated, single, widowed). Then, since some studies measured only married or unmarried values, the values from the segmented unmarried values were collapsed into one category — unmarried. Thus, married was then compared to unmarried.

Coding category five: Education. In some studies, respondents were asked to state the highest grade obtained (fill-in-the-blank). In order to accommodate all studies into one coding scheme, four responses were chosen.

Coding category six: Employment Status. Many surveys employed separate questions in their determination of the respondent's employment status. Other studies included employment status as a component of the income source question. After reviewing all the surveys, eleven descriptors were chosen for this category.

Coding category seven: Income. The data was normalized prior to comparison, because of the inconsistency of questioning from survey to survey. Mean household size was calculated or obtained from each individual survey (see Category Nine). Mean household income was computed by determining the numerical midpoint of the income range and multiplying by n for each range. The mean was then calculated from these numbers. Then, using the U.S. Census Bureaus' Poverty Guidelines, the 100 percent of poverty level and the 125 percent of poverty level for the specific year and household size were determined. The percentage of the respondents falling below the 100 percent and the 125 percent poverty levels was determined for each survey.

Coding category eight: Income Source. This category contains the largest number of descriptors. Employment status was addressed in Coding Category Six and, therefore, is only viewed here as income from "salaries". The descriptor of "other" pertains to unusual sources of income such as bottle-collecting.

Coding category nine: Household Size. For Category Nine, a mean household size was computed for each study. Household size was not allowed to exceed six in the determination of household size. Since relatively few values were greater than six, on any survey, it was deemed appropriate to have the 6+ descriptor. This maximum value was adopted because many of the surveys employed a response of "household size greater than six".

Coding category ten: Household Composition. The presence of children in a household is an important determinant of hunger risk. Furthermore, the number of adults in a household is also an important factor in determining the composition of households experiencing hunger. Therefore, the four descriptors listed in Table 1 are adequate to determine household composition for this study.

Coding category eleven: Special Dietary Needs. Very few surveys questioned respondents as to the need for a special diet. Of the studies that did inquire, four descriptors emerged as representative of the types of questions asked by surveys.

Coding category twelve: Food Stamp Participation. The five questions (descriptors) chosen for Table 1, are representative of the Food Stamp Program participation questions that were present in the surveys. These questions determined whether or not respondents were receiving food stamps, if individuals were experiencing shortages of food stamps, and if they had experienced difficulty in obtaining food stamps.

Coding category thirteen: Participation in Other Government Food Assistance Programs. Category thirteen lists the five main government food assistance programs, other than the Food Stamp Program. Frequently, the information about participation in food assistance programs was contained in other question areas (e.g., income source).

Coding category fourteen: Participation in Government Assistance Programs. Each study was reviewed in order to ascertain which government assistance programs are of importance to hunger researchers. This information was used to determine the descriptors for this category. As noted in Category Thirteen, information about participation was found in other question areas (e.g., income source).

Coding category fifteen: Hunger Perception. Surveys were reviewed to determine whether or not respondents were questioned as to their perceived state of hunger. Three areas of questions (see Table 1) consistently appeared in surveys that addressed this topic.

Coding category sixteen: Living Conditions. Determination of access to cooking facilities is the main goal of this question area. Descriptors in this category are designed to measure access to cooking facilities. This type of access has been purported to be linked to hunger.

It should be noted that every survey did not answer in every category. This is acknowledged by the author and compensated for in the statistical analysis section.

Coding category seventeen: Geographic location. Descriptors in this category are designed to discover the region of the country in which the individual resides. Geographic location is determined using government regions such as those used by the Internal Revenue Service. This category also records the type of locale (urban, rural, or suburban) in which the respondent resides.

The Survey Weighting System

The Survey Weighting System was developed in order to provide a standard format to credit surveys for their use of superior methods, procedures, instruments and reporting. Weighting is a critical, but often neglected component of meta-analysis.

Studies were reviewed for their use of the generally accepted survey principles of sampling technique, study design (including the survey instrument and administration of the survey), hunger perception measurement, and method of reporting. Surveys adhering to accepted principles of survey methodological technique were awarded higher weighting point values than studies which were poorly designed and/or conducted. Weighting scores from the two readers were averaged to produce one weighting score. This score was then used in the data analysis section in order to compute the weighted statistics. Table 2 depicts the weighting categories, subcategories, and assigned point values.

Weighting category one: Sample. For this category there were three subcategories and a maximum number of three points that a survey could obtain. One point was assigned to surveys that used an appropriate sample size for the population being studied. Studies in which a random sample from the entire population had been drawn received two points, whereas surveys that drew a sample from a pre-selected population were awarded one point. An example of a pre-selected random population is a random sample from the entire population of recipients from a specific food bank.

Weighting category two: Survey Design. All surveys that pilot-tested the survey were granted two points. Another point was awarded to surveys that asked questions in a clear and reasonable fashion. Surveys employing multiple questions in the determination of a variable were allotted one point. Training interviewers and continuity of administration result in more reliable data collection and, therefore, were each assigned one weighting point. Surveys written by or conducted by nationally recognized hunger research groups were also awarded one point.

Weighting category three: Hunger Perception Measurement. Category Three assigned weighting to studies in which the perception of respondent's hunger was measured. A maximum of four points was possible in this category. One point was awarded for surveys that attempted any measure of hunger perception. For the inclusion of each of the three questions from Category 15 of Table 1 the survey received one third of a point. Studies using some quantifiable non-physical measure of hunger (e.g., the number of meals per week missed because of lack of food) were assigned an additional point. Finally, studies in which a physiological or anthropometric measure of hunger were conducted were granted one point.

Table 2: The Survey Weighting System

WEIGHTING	SUBCATEGORIES	POINTS
1: Sample	Appropriate sample size	1
	Random sample from population	2
	Random sample from pre-selected population	1
2: Survey Design	Survey pilot-tested	2
	Question Clarity	1
	Multiple questions asked in determination of a variable	1
	Interviewers trained	1
	Continuity of Administration	1
	Standard survey	1
3: Hunger Perception	Survey used hunger measurement	1
	Asked: "Are you hungry"	1/3
	Asked: "Did any family member skip a meal due to lack of food"	1/3
	Asked: "Do children go to bed hungry"	1/3
	Attempted to quantify a response	1
	Physical/anthropometric measure	1
4: Reporting Method	Underwent peer review (refereed journal)	2
	Dissertation	1
	Supplied the testing instrument	1
	Accuracy of numerical tabulation	1
	Reported in scientific format	1
	Quality of description procedure	1

Weighting category four: Method of Reporting. The final category of weighting was the method of reporting. Publication of a study in a refereed journal signifies its scientific validity and, therefore, studies appearing in such journals were assumed to be of a higher caliber than unpublished studies. Published studies, then, were awarded two points. Appearance of a hunger study in a dissertation identifies the study as one that has been subjected to intense scrutiny. Therefore, surveys designed as part of a doctoral dissertation or master's thesis were assigned a point value of one. Surveys that included the original testing instrument earned one point because these surveys could be properly assessed by the researcher. Accuracy of numerical tabulations refers to proper computations involving numbers and percentages in the study. One point was allotted for accurate mathematics. Studies reporting findings in a readable, scientific fashion received one point. Studies in which procedures were clearly delineated received one point. A maximum of six points could be received in this weighting category and twenty points was a perfect overall score.

IV

Results and Discussion

In this chapter, the results and discussion relative to the quantitative analysis of the data set are presented. The statistical techniques utilized are the first points of discussion. In the next section, the study sample is briefly described. The results of the quantitative portion of the meta-analysis are used to describe the socio-demographic characteristics of the sample population. These characteristics are also discussed as they vary according to survey site and survey type. Finally, correlational analyses are examined. The correlations between selected variables and the hunger perception index are first discussed. Then, the correlational analyses among the 17 coded categorical variables are described and discussed.

STATISTICAL ANALYSES

After an unweighted analysis, data (in proportions) was weighted first using the rating techniques described in the previous chapter and then weighted using the principles of sampling theory. Each weighted data set was analyzed for descriptive statistics and Pearson product-moment correlation coefficients. Due to insufficient cell sizes, the more sophisticated statistical techniques of logistic regression, multiple regression analysis, discriminant analysis, and canonical analysis could not be performed. These small cell sizes were attributed to the extreme variability in the nature and manner in which data was collected for the studies included in the investigation.

Descriptive Analysis

Descriptive statistics for this analysis included the following measurements: frequency counts, means, modes, medians, standard deviations, variances, minimum and maximum values, ranges, and sums. Mean scores, standard deviations, minimum, maximum, and sample sizes were the summary statistics used in this study. Summary statistics for the unweighted proportions, meta-analysis weighted proportions, and sampling theory weighted proportions were computed. A central tendency is indicated by the mean and the variability for each proportion is indicated by its associated standard deviation.

Correlational Analysis

The Pearson product-moment correlation was used to examine the relationship between pairs of variables from the 17 coding categories described in Chapter Three. The correlation coefficient provides an indication of the strength of the linear relationship between the two variables. Associations which cannot exist by chance alone are said to be statistically significant at the .05 level (for 95% of the cases) or at the .01 level (for 99% of the cases).

Meta-Analysis Weighting

The meta-analysis weighting was devised to give statistical consideration to survey strength. Surveys were examined for measures of reliability and validity using a scale explained in detail in Chapter Three. Two raters reviewed each study in order to give greater reliability to the raters scores. The raters were chosen for their familiarity with hunger research in the United States and for their knowledge of survey methodology. The inter-rater reliability coefficient indicates the level of equivalence of the information obtained by the raters. In this study the coefficient reflects the level of agreement between the two raters with regard to the weighting of the 27 hunger surveys. The inter-rater reliability for the survey weightings was a Pearson product-moment correlation coefficient of 0.89. This statistic reflects a high level of consistency between the two raters.

Weighting occurred according to the number of cases and the ratio of the weight to the sum of the weights. These weighted values were used for the Pearson product-moment correlation analyses.

Sampling Theory Weighting

Sampling theory was used as the basis of one of the weighted analyses considered in this study. This technique gave greater merit to studies with large sample size. The study with the greatest sample size, then, received the highest weighting. Because of the tremendous disparity in the sample size of the Minnesota survey of 13,176 respondents, however, the information from the sampling theory weighting was not used.

Scatterplot Analysis

Scatterplot analysis was used to determine possible relationships between hunger variables and all other variables. This analysis was used to examine the relationships between variables particularly when it was not possible to use Pearson product-moment correlation analyses due to insufficient cell sizes. The scatterplot analysis was used specifically to examine the linearity between variables of interest in this study. In addition, it was utilized to isolate outlying data points which may have influenced the results of the Pearson product-moment correlation analyses.

DESCRIPTION OF THE SAMPLE

The description of the study sample will include a discussion of the methods of survey discovery as well as a discussion of the characteristics of the selected surveys. This discussion focuses on the survey types, survey sources, locales, regions, and years of the surveys.

Method of Discovery

The statistical portion of this study is based on 27 surveys that were selected for inclusion in the study. Using the three strategies for the discovery of hunger studies delineated in Chapter Three, 158 hunger studies were discovered and obtained. Strategy two (examination of FRAC files) produced the most studies. An attempt was made to collect data from studies that met all criteria, but were lacking appropriate data sets. After thorough examination of the surveys, 27 were chosen for quantitative analysis because they met the sample criteria. These 27 studies chosen for examination are listed in the appendix.

Characteristics of the Sample

The 27 studies examined in the quantitative portion of the analysis varied greatly for some factors, but failed to show as wide a variance for others. The characteristics of the selected surveys are depicted in Table 3. Prior to selection of the surveys, but after review of the 158 studies, certain survey characteristics were identified. For instance, four survey types were recognized—personal interview, questionnaire, mailing, and phone survey. Twenty of the surveys used in this analysis were interviews conducted by researchers at the assistance sites. The remaining seven surveys were administered as written questionnaires. None of the mailed questionnaires or phone interview surveys met the selection criteria.

Collection sites/population types. After examination of all hunger surveys, nine types of collection sites or population types were determined. These nine types include the following: food pantry, soup kitchen, government commodity distribution site, food pantry and soup kitchen, food pantry and soup kitchen and government commodity distribution site, social service agency, emergency assistance site, general population samples, and low income population samples. Seven of these site collection types were represented by the surveys selected for inclusion in the quantitative analysis. The majority of surveys (63%) were conducted exclusively either at food pantries or at some combination of food pantries and soup kitchens.

Table 3: Characteristics of the Surveys Included
in the Statistical Analysis

Survey Characteristics	n	Percent
Food Pantry	9	33.3
Soup Kitchen	1	3.7
Food Pantry & Soup Kitchen	8	29.6
Emergency Assistance Sites	5	7.4
Social Service Agency	2	18.5
Population	1	3.7
Low-income	1	3.7
Survey Type		
Interview	20	74.1
Survey	7	25.9
Year		
1983	1	3.7
1984	4	14.8
1985	4	14.8
1986	4	14.8
1987	3	11.1
1988	2	7.4
1989	9	33.3
Locale		
Urban	10	37.0
Suburban	2	7.4
Rural	2	7.4
Urban and Rural	7	25.9
Unknown	6	22.2

Table 3: Characteristics of the Surveys Included
in the Statistical Analysis

Survey Characteristics	n	Percent
Region		
Region 1 CT, ME, MA, NH, RI, VT	1	3.7
Region 2 NJ, NY	10	37.0
Region 3 DE, DC, MD, PA, VA, WV	1	3.7
Region 4 AL, FL, GA, KY, MS NC, SC, TN	1	3.7
Region 5 IL, IN, MI, MN, OH, WI	5	18.5
Region 6 AK, LA, NM, OK, TX	1	3.7
Region 7 IA, KS, MO, NE	1	3.7
Region 8 CO, MT, ND, SD, UT, WY	1	3.7
Region 9 CA, HI, NV	4	14.8
Region 10 AL, ID, OR, WA	2	7.4
National	0	

Locale. Studies were also examined for the type of locale in which the survey was conducted. It was determined that surveys were conducted in one of five areas—urban, suburban, rural, urban and rural, or unknown. Urban surveys accounted for 37% of the sample. An unusually large percentage of the sample (22%) had locales categorized as "unknown." This was the case because many studies did not accurately describe the locale in which the survey was performed. In some cases, it was necessary to determine the study locale through contact with the agency conducting the original survey.

Geographic locale. Geographic locale was categorized based on ten regions of the country. One category was established for national studies. These regions (by state) are defined in Table 3. The largest percentage of surveys used in this study came from Region 2 (i.e., New York and New Jersey). More of the surveys conducted in this region met the survey selection criterion. Additionally, New York State has probably the most advanced system of monitoring and reporting of hunger problems in the United States. Therefore, a larger number of useable surveys were conducted in this region.

Survey sample size. The range for the number of individuals responding to each of the surveys varied greatly. The smallest number of participants in a given survey was 32, and the largest number was 13,176. The mean survey sample size was 1277, the standard deviation was 2513, the median was 446, and the sum was 34,469. These results, however, are tremendously skewed by the case which had 13,176 respondents. The "n" for each survey is listed in the appendix.

SOCIO-DEMOGRAPHIC CHARACTERISTICS

As noted previously, three sets of descriptive statistics were computed (unweighted, sampling theory weighted, and meta-analysis weighted). Only the meta-analysis weighted scores were used in the following description of the characteristics of individuals seeking emergency food assistance.

Gender and Age

Overall, 61% of individuals participating in the surveys were women and 39% were men. The actual mean age of the sample was 38.4 years. The calculated (or artificial) mean was 39.0 years of age.

Ethnic Group

The majority of the participants (51%) reported that they are white. Of the remaining 49%, the overwhelming majority were Black (32%). Hispanics comprised 11% of the group, followed by American Indians with 4%, Asians with 1%, and the remaining 1% belonging to other ethnic groups.

Marital Status

Married individuals comprised 32% of the respondents. Of the remaining 68%, 30% reported to be single, 26% divorced or separated, 8% were widowed, and 4% were cohabiting.

Education

Only 17% of the participants reported to have education beyond the level of a high school diploma. Of the remaining 83%, 48% reported never having earned a high school diploma or its equivalent.

Employment status

In the discussion of employment status it should be noted that the percentages did not total 100%. This was due to the fact that individuals may have received income from more than one of the employment sources. Unemployment was reported by 54% of the survey respondents. Full-time positions were held by 20% of the employed respondents and 14% held part-time positions. Retired individuals accounted for 13% of respondents and 20% reported that they were disabled. The categories of temporary, seasonal, and more than one part-time job had insufficient cases to generate descriptive statistics. Eighteen percent of respondents stated that their spouse was employed and 12% stated that they held "other employment."

Income

Of those individuals responding to income level questions, 75% received incomes placing them in the 100% of poverty level or below. Individuals in the 125% of poverty level (or below) comprised 83% of those responding to the question.

Income source

Income source is another category in which an overlap between the descriptors produced percentages that did not add to zero. An individual, for instance, may have reported more than one income source. Participation in the food stamp program was reported by 49% of the respondents, 3% reported income from pensions and retirement, 29% received funds from AFDC, 18% reported income from general assistance, 16% listed money from gifts as an income source, 12% received income from social security disability benefits, and 15% received benefits from social security retirement income. Receipt of home relief was reported by 13%, 26% reported income from salaries, 12% received supplemental security income, 4% received disability/workers' compensation, and 8% reported that they received no income whatsoever. It is interesting to note that only 1% of respondents reported the receipt of alimony and only 5% reported the receipt of child support.

Household size

The majority of households (69%) had more than one resident. Households consisting of two individuals constituted 19% of the sample, households of three individuals accounted for 16% of the sample, households containing four persons accounted for 14% of the households, 9% of the households consisted of five individuals, and 10% of the sample reported a household size of six or more.

Household Composition

The term household composition refers to the number of children, elderly persons, and/or adults residing within the household. Households that contained single adults and no children represented 34% of the sample. Households with two adults and no children accounted for 16% of sample participants who responded to this question. Of the 52% of the households with children, 46% were inhabited by one adult and 54% had more than one adult living within the residence. The average number of children per household was 2.3 and the average age of these children was 7.85 years. Seventeen percent of households contained elderly individuals.

Special Dietary Needs

In some surveys investigators questioned participants about special dietary considerations of household members. Of those responding to this question, 23% answered that a special diet is required for someone in their household. None of the respondents reported that they or any member of their family had been treated for a hunger-related illness such as anemia. Pregnant or lactating women resided in 6% of the households. Five percent of respondents required a diet low in sugar, 5% required a low salt diet, 4% required a low fat diet, and 10% reported that they had "other" special dietary needs. It was not determined what "other" comprises, but it should be noted that in some studies this may have referred to pregnant or lactating women.

Food Stamp Participation

Food stamp participation was investigated in all of the 27 studies. Not all studies, however, measured all descriptors in this category. Food stamps were received in 49% of the households. Food stamps did not last the entire month for 71% of food stamp recipients. The average number of months that families had been receiving food stamps was 17. Questions designed to determine past receipt of food stamps and reasons for non-receipt in the present, did not generate adequate data for analysis.

Participation in Other Government FoodAssistance Programs

School Lunch was received by 28% of the households and 17% received School Breakfast. At the time of the survey, 14% reported the current receipt of benefits from the WIC program, 39% were receiving surplus commodities, and 4% benefitted from the head start feeding program. Meals on Wheels were received by 1% of the respondents and 3% reported receiving Congregate meals. It was impossible to ascertain the percent of eligibility for these programs because of lack of appropriate data.

Participation in Government Assistance Programs

Respondents were also asked to report participation in government assistance programs. Beneficiaries of Medicaid comprised 50% of the sample and 65% reported household members who were receiving Medicare benefits. This high value for Medicare use is probably due to respondents' confusion between Medicare and Medicaid. As noted previously, 29% of respondents in this sample were receiving AFDC benefits. Many of the descriptors measured in the "source of income" category were also measured in this category. Differences between the percentages are small and, therefore, can be attributed to some type of interpretive error either by respondents or researchers.

Hunger Perception

The measurement of hunger was judged, by this researcher, to be an important element of the hunger surveys, yet the measurement was attempted in only 18 of the 27 surveys. Hunger was reported by 48% of the individuals questioned about the existence of hunger in their household. Skipping meals because of lack of food occurred in 43% of households that reported hunger in the household. In 36% of the households reporting hunger, children sometimes went without food because of lack of an adequate supply.

Living Conditions

Homeless individuals in this study comprised 10% of the total sample. Home ownership was reported by 10% of the respondents, 79% of respondents were tenants, 5% lived with relatives, and 8% reported other types of living arrangements. Access to cooking facilities was reported by 82% of individuals answering this question while 12% stated that they had no cooking facilities.

Characteristics by Assistance Site

Nine surveys were conducted exclusively at food pantries and eight surveys were conducted at combined food pantry/soup kitchen sites. Very small case numbers for some of the variables studied made comparison of some characteristics of individuals impossible because outliers had too pronounced an effect on the data. In some instances, there were sufficient case numbers to allow further discussion of these variables. When standard deviations were taken into account, however, there was very little variation between the proportion means.

Some notable exceptions occurred when large differences were noted and when the number of cases increased. In the case of School Lunch, for instance, there may have been an increased participation rate for individuals at food pantries over those in the mixed sample (food pantry and soup kitchen). This difference was also noted for eligibility for the School Lunch program.

Individuals in the food pantry/soup kitchen group were three times more likely to report hunger than those in the food pantry group. In fact, individuals surveyed at the food pantry/soup kitchen sites had percentage scores that far exceeded those at food pantry sites for all hunger perception variables. It appears that food pantry/soup kitchen respondents were hungrier than food pantry respondents. This may be true because of a larger use of soup kitchens than food pantries by homeless people. Access to cooking facilities is also a problem for the homeless, so foodstuffs from food pantries are not in high demand by the homeless population.

Characteristics by Survey Type

Although there were many survey types employed by hunger researchers in the 1980s, only two survey types were represented in the sample set. Of the 27 surveys selected for inclusion in the quantitative portion of this study, 20 were conducted through a verbal interview at the assistance site. The remaining seven surveys were conducted by written questionnaires administered at the food assistance site. Again, as in the comparison of emergency food assistance sites, small case numbers made the comparison of the two survey types difficult.

Eighty-five percent of individuals questioned by written questionnaire and 72% of individuals questioned by interview reported incomes which placed them in the 100% of poverty level or below. For income level of 125% of poverty level or below, individuals in 92% of the households questioned by written survey were living at this level. For individuals in the interview group, this value was 81%. The disparity in income level could be due to the method of reporting, but the small case size number does not preclude that the disagreement is artificial in nature. Whatever the method of the interview, however, it is clear that the individuals answering the income question at food assistance sites were impoverished people.

A large difference was noted in the ethnicity category. The percentage of individuals who reported to be white and those who reported to be American Indians increased for the written questionnaire. This percentage diminished for Black individuals and nonwhite individuals. Given the small number of cases, the survey with the largest number of participants may have skewed the results. Indeed, the largest study conducted was a written questionnaire.

Less employment was reported by respondents to written surveys than by respondents to personal interviews. Food stamp use was relatively similar, yet there was a slight increase in participation rates for written questionnaire respondents. Participation in the WIC program was exactly the same for both survey types. School Lunch was used less by individuals responding to written questionnaires. The interview surveys counted more homeless respondents than the written surveys.

Summary

Respondents in this study were predominantly female and about 38 years-old. A little over one-half of the respondents were white and one-third were Black. Most participants were unmarried and a little less than one-half of the sample had never finished high school. Most of those responding indicated that they were living below the 100% of poverty level. More than one half of the respondents queried indicated that they were unemployed. Most households had more than one resident (69%), tended to rent their dwelling, and had some access to cooking facilities. Approximately one-half of the respondents reported the receipt of food stamps. In households where children were present, the average number of children was 2.3 and the average age of the children was 7.85 years.

Special diets were required by at least one individual in 23% of households reporting for this variable. Households tended to use other government assistance and food assistance programs. Medicaid was reportedly used by 50% of the respondents and Medicare was used by 65% of respondents. Little less than one-third were receiving AFDC. Hunger was attributed to a lack of food by 43% of those asked. Children went hungry in one-third of the households. Very little difference was seen between the survey types and assistance sites, although there was some indication that individuals at soup kitchens may have been more hungry than individuals seeking emergency assistance at food pantries.

Individuals in this sample, those people who sought emergency food assistance in the 1980s, show a definite thread of unity. The recipients of food assistance were, for the most part, tenants, unemployed, poorly educated and living in poverty. Surprisingly enough, many were using some form of government food assistance or relied on government benefits for at least a portion of their income. In addition, an alarming number of households with children reported that their children went hungry.

CORRELATIONAL ANALYSES

This section examines the Pearson product-moment correlations for pairs of variables. The first part of the section is devoted to a discussion of how each of the Coded Categorical Variables described in Chapter Three are correlated with the six variables from the hunger perception coding category. Second, the correlation coefficients for all variables (except those from the hunger perception category) are discussed category by category.

Hunger Perception

Pearson product-moment correlation analyses were used to assess the relationship among the three hunger perception descriptors (i.e., individuals who say they are hungry, households where meals are skipped, and households in which children go without food) and all other Coded Categorical Variables. These analyses were conducted in an effort to discover variables that were associated with hunger in this sample group. The Pearson product-moment correlations for each pair of variables were calculated using the meta-analysis weighted proportions. Correlation coefficients which were significant at .05 and .01 levels are discussed below. Because of the small number of cases involved in some of the correlations, not all significant relationships may have been identified by the Pearson product-moment correlation analyses. Therefore, the scatter plots for these variables were examined in order to identify possible relationships among the variables. Relationships which may be linear were also examined.

Gender/Sex. For the coding category of gender only one significant correlation was revealed. A negative correlation was discovered between women, in this sample, and individuals who stated that they were not hungry. An analysis of the scatterplot indicated that a significant relationship may have occurred between males and individuals who reported that they did not skip meals because of lack of food. Males in this sample, therefore, may have been more hungry than females or were more likely to seek this type of emergency food assistance.

Ethnic group. Several significant correlations were revealed for ethnicities. A positive correlation coefficient was calculated for the variable "no meals were skipped" and white individuals. For nonwhite, Asian, and Black individuals, an analysis of the scatter plots indicated a possible negative association for these variables and "no meals were skipped." A significant correlation for the variable "no meals were skipped" and Hispanic ethnicity existed. These correlations suggest that white individuals were less likely to skip meals than nonwhite individuals.

The correlation coefficient for the question "Do your children have food?" was significant and negative for nonwhite individuals. An analysis of the scatterplot revealed that the correlation for this hunger perception variable and whites may have been significant. This implies that white individuals were more likely to state that their children had adequate food. For this same variable, an examination of significant correlations and scatter plots revealed that, of the nonwhite population, American Indians and Asians were more likely to report that their children had food.

A negative correlation existed between individuals who reported that they skipped meals because of lack of food and members of the Asian population. Asians, then, were less likely to skip meals because of lack of food. While these results could be spurious in nature, this issue merits further examination. Some type of access problem based on ethnicity may be at work here.

Marital status. No significant correlations existed for any of the hunger perception variables and any of the marital status variables.

Education. No significant correlations were found nor any linear relationships identified for any of the hunger variables and the educational level variables.

Employment status. A significant negative correlation coefficient for employment and the variable "meals are skipped" existed. Individuals who were employed, therefore, were not likely to skip meals.

A positive correlation was discovered for individuals who reported that their children did not have food and had part-time employment. An analysis of the scatterplot revealed that there may have been an association between full-time employment and children who did have food. As a result of this finding, it can be implied that a relationship existed between employment and an individual's ability to adequately feed the children.

Income. Examination of the scatter plots revealed a possible linear relationship between both poverty levels and skipping meals. Being in either poverty level, however, was significantly associated with children being fed. This relationship seems incongruent with the supposition that people in poverty have difficulty obtaining adequate food. As income level decreased, however, the strength of these relationships increased, thus indicating that income level did have an impact on the hunger variables in this study.

Income source. The correlation coefficient for the variables "children do not have food" and the receipt of general assistance benefits was significant and positive. This implies that individuals receiving general assistance benefits had difficulty in adequately feeding their children.

Home relief and hunger were positively associated. Furthermore, a positive correlation occurred between the receipt of home relief and hungry children. It can be inferred from these correlations that there was a relationship between the receipt of home relief and being hungry. It appears that the receipt of home relief does not provide enough income to meet basic needs.

A positive correlation existed between individuals who expressed the receipt of gifts as an income source and those who skipped meals because of a lack of food. It can be suggested, therefore, that there was some relationship between hunger and reliance upon gifts for income. This may indicate a reliance by some of these individuals on friends and relatives.

The use of pensions or retirement as an income source and hungry children were negatively associated. Scatterplot analysis indicated a negative correlation between hungry children and social security retirement income. The implication is that children who resided in households in which retirement benefits were received as a source of income, were not hungry. This result may be due to the small cell size. It may also indicate a number of children who reside with grandparents.

The receipt of veterans' benefits as an income source and skipping meals were positively correlated. This may indicate that veteran's benefits were too low. Based on this finding, veterans' benefits may be too low to insure adequate funds for food purchases.

The scatterplot analysis revealed a possible linearity between salary as an income source and not skipping meals. The receipt of a salary may have provided some protection from hunger. This may indicate that wages were insufficient to meet basic needs so individuals, in this sample, sought emergency food assistance

Household size. A negative correlation was observed for a household size of one and the variable "do not skip meals." For all other household sizes this correlation was positive, but not significant. This suggests those single individuals living alone were more likely to skip meals because of lack of food. This finding may reflect a large component of homeless individuals in the sample.

Household size of four was correlated with skipping meals and the presence of hunger. However, children in these households were not hungry. This may indicate that School Lunch and breakfast programs were used or that adults gave their food to their children.

Household composition. A negative association was found between the variables of "meals skipped" and "two adults/no children." According to the scatterplot, a negative association may have existed for a household consisting of two adults and no children and hunger. Based on these associations, it may be implied that hunger may have occurred in households containing two adults and no children. An examination of the scatter plots also revealed a possible association between single adults with children and hunger and also for single adults with children and skipping meals. A negative correlation coefficient, however, existed for households with children and children not having food. Hunger, therefore, may have been a problem in single adult households in which children were present.

Special dietary needs. Hunger and pregnancy (i.e., a pregnant individual resided in the household) were significantly correlated. A correlation was found between households with pregnant women and households that reported skipping meals. This implies that pregnant women were hungry or that members of households occupied by pregnant women went without food. An examination of the reasons for nonparticipation in the WIC program should be undertaken.

Food stamp participation. A positive correlation coefficient was calculated for the receipt of food stamps and the variable "do not skip meals." This may indicate that food stamps were effective in alleviating hunger. Positive correlations were revealed for households reporting that food stamps did not last the entire month and households reporting skipped meals. Households in which individuals reported hunger and households reporting that food stamps did not last the entire month also had a positive correlation coefficient. It can be implied, therefore, that food stamps did not ameliorate the problem of hunger when they did not last until month's end.

Participation in other government food assistance programs. A strong positive association occurred for School Lunch program eligibility and hungry children. This suggests that children in these households should have used School Lunch to alleviate their hunger. It may also be interpreted that students may have received School Lunch but still skipped meals at home.

An examination of the scatterplots revealed a possible negative correlation between skipping meals and participation in the Meals on Wheels program. This suggests that participants in this program did not skip meals as often as people who did not participate in the program.

Participation in government assistance programs. A positive association was identified between individuals receiving social security disability income and hunger. A positive correlation coefficient was calculated for the variables "receipt of general assistance benefits" and "children do not have food." It can be suggested, therefore, that receipt of funds from either of these programs did not negate the risk of hunger. This may indicate that benefit levels for these programs were too low to provide for basic living needs.

Living conditions. A significant correlation was revealed between being hungry and the "live other" variable. These individuals may have been homeless or living in shelters. Hunger and not being homeless were negatively associated.

An analysis of scatterplots indicated possible associations between being homeless and children not having food and renting and children not having food. The scatterplot analyses also revealed a possible negative association between the lack of cooking facilities and children having food. This information suggests that the homeless, tenants, and those who lacked cooking facilities had difficulty feeding their children.

Summary. Although small case numbers for some of the variables inhibited this analysis, some interesting correlations were discovered. Whites, as well as their children, were less likely to be hungry than nonwhites. Full-time employment seems to have reduced the risk of hunger for both children and adults in this sample. Hunger, in this sample, was associated with unemployment, with part-time employment, and with the receipt of income that was not in the form of a salary. Income from gifts, home relief, general assistance and veteran's benefits were all positively associated with hunger. The receipt of AFDC benefits and social security disability income benefits did not negate hunger.

Other individuals residing in households may have sacrificed in order to insure that at-risk groups residing in their own households were protected. Households with children may have fed children first. Pregnant women may have also been protected. Food stamp participation probably alleviated hunger, but when households ran out of food stamps that protection was diminished and hunger reappeared.

Correlations for Coded Categorical Variables

All descriptor variables for all coding categories were paired and Pearson product-moment correlations for each pair of variables were calculated using the meta-analysis weighted proportions. Correlation coefficients which were significant at the .05 and .01 levels of significance are of interest and importance. Observations in the rest of this chapter are based on these Pearson product-moment correlations.

Gender/Sex. The correlation coefficient for males and the nonwhite variable was positive and significant. A positive correlation between being female and being white existed. This information implies that the male respondents participating in this survey were predominantly nonwhite, whereas females participating in the study were more likely to be white. A positive correlation between males and Hispanics and a negative correlation between females and Hispanics suggests that, of Hispanic participants in the surveys, the majority were males.

Two interesting correlations existed between marital status and gender. There was a positive correlation between females and individuals who were divorced, separated, or single. For males and the variable "divorced or separated" this correlation was negative. A negative correlation existed for males and a positive correlation for females with the variable "single." Women in this study, then, were more likely to be single, divorced, or separated than men in this study.

A positive correlation was determined for females and failure to receive a high school diploma. Among males, this association was negative. Additionally, the correlation of males and education beyond high school resulted in a positive value. For females, and this same variable the association was negative. Correlation coefficients suggest that females, in this sample, were less educated than male respondents.

The correlation between food stamps and males resulted in a negative value, whereas for females the association was positive. It appears, from this information, that women received food stamps more often than men. A later set of correlations adds credence to this supposition. The correlation coefficient for males who received food stamps (in the category "participation in food stamp programs") was negative. For females this association was positive.

For correlations between household size and gender, a number of statistically significant correlations were recorded. The statistical analyses revealed a positive correlation for males and a negative correlation for females with a household size of one. This suggests that, of single individuals seeking food assistance, the majority were men. Examination of correlation coefficients for the household composition variable "single/no children" and gender, provided evidence to support this assumption.

For females and household sizes more than one, all correlations were positive. These correlations were negative for males. For households consisting of two adults with children present, there was a positive association with females and a negative association with males. This implies that female-headed families were more likely to seek food at emergency assistance sites.

Full-time employment was positively associated with being male and part-time employment was negatively associated with being male. Computed correlation coefficients for employment and gender indicated that males represented more of the full-time employed individuals than females. Inverse values were calculated for females and these variables.

For gender and income source variables, many interesting associations were discovered. The receipt of AFDC, child support and Medicaid were all positively correlated with being female. These values were negative for men. The receipt of veterans' benefits and the declaration of "no income" were positively associated with males. These values seem appropriate since women typically receive more AFDC, child support and Medicaid services than men, whereas males are more likely to receive veterans' benefits than women.

A number of interesting correlations between variables in the gender category and those in the category of participation in government food assistance programs were discovered. As noted previously, receiving food stamps and being female were positively associated. Female gender and both WIC eligibility and WIC participation were significantly correlated. These correlation coefficients were negative for men. Since WIC can only be used by women and children, the results appear valid. Males responding to a survey, however, may have responded that a female in their household was a WIC participant. This accounts for the fact that this value is not perfectly linear. It should be noted that the correlation coefficient for females and WIC eligibility was larger than that for WIC participation. This suggests that there may have been individuals who were eligible for, but not participating in, the WIC program.

There was a positive association between children participating in the School Lunch program and women. This correlation coefficient was reversed for men. This implies that females were more likely to have children who participated in School Lunch programs. The fact that the males may not be reporting that children residing in their household are receiving School Lunch may not be accounted for in this finding.

The correlation coefficient of males and being homeless was positive. For females this relationship was negative. Homeless people who seek emergency food assistance, therefore, are more likely to be men.

A positive correlation between females and owning a home existed. It can be suggested, therefore, that among individuals seeking emergency food assistance, home ownership was most likely to occur among females.

Ethnic group. As noted previously, it appeared that males in this sample were more likely to be nonwhite and Hispanics in the sample were more likely to be males. There was a negative correlation between the 125% of poverty level and being Hispanic, but a positive correlation between this level of poverty and being Asian. The same was true at the 100% of poverty level, yet the strength of the correlations was diminished.

A positive correlation between being married and being Hispanic and a negative correlation between Hispanic ethnicity and being divorced or separated suggests that Hispanic respondents were more likely to be married than non-Hispanic respondents.

For the category of the level of education attained and ethnicity, a number of interesting correlations were revealed. A positive correlation coefficient was calculated for being nonwhite and having education beyond the high school diploma whereas there was a negative association between being white and having an education beyond high school. Hispanics had a strong positive correlation coefficient with education beyond high school and a strong negative correlation with less than a high school degree. Being Asian and possessing a high school diploma was positively associated. These correlations suggest that Hispanics in this sample tended to be highly educated and Asians tended to have a high school education.

In this particular sample, being Asian and being employed was strongly positively correlated. Similarly, a strong negative correlation was determined for Asian ethnicity and unemployment. Thus suggesting that, of individuals who were employed, a disproportionate number were of Asian descent. Full-time employment and Hispanic ethnicity were strongly correlated whereas full-time employment and being white were negatively correlated. This implies that, of Hispanics who were employed, more had full-time jobs than part-time jobs. The same correlation, although not as strong, existed for American Indians.

A number of interesting correlations were revealed for ethnicity and income source variables. Pensions appeared to be received most often by whites in the sample, since this correlation existed between whites and pensions. Social security retirement income and unemployment compensation were also positively correlated with being white and negatively correlated with being nonwhite. The existence of a negative correlation coefficient between Blacks and receipt of pensions, suggests that nonwhites who were not receiving pensions were more likely to be Black. Nonwhite individuals and Black individuals and the receipt of veterans' benefits were positively correlated. As a result of a negative correlation between American Indians and the receipt of disability or worker's compensation it can be implied that American Indians, for whatever reason, did not receive as many of these benefits as other groups.

Earlier it was disclosed that employment and Asian ethnicity were positively correlated. A positive correlation was found between Asians and income from salary. Correlation coefficients for full-time employment indicated an association with Hispanics. Individuals in the "no income" category were likely to be Hispanic. It appears that most Hispanics had either full-time employment or no income.

A positive association for a household size of one existed for nonwhites, Blacks, and Hispanics. In the household composition category of "single/no children," an association was discovered for nonwhites, Blacks, and Hispanics. It appears that single individuals in this sample, were nonwhite, and were likely to be Black or Hispanic.

Based on several positive correlations it can be suggested that households with children, in this sample, were predominantly white. The variables "households with children" and "two adults with children residing in the household" produced positive values when correlated with the variable "white." In addition, household sizes of two, three, and five individuals were significantly associated with being white.

In the categories of the receipt of food stamps and participation in other government food assistance programs a number of significant correlations were revealed. A negative value was produced for the association between food stamp use and both Hispanics and American Indians. The value was positive when the variable "Hispanic" was compared to the variable "no food stamps received." As a result of these correlations it can be suggested that Hispanics and American Indians, in this sample, were less likely to use food stamps than members of other groups.

WIC eligibility was negatively associated with both nonwhites and Blacks. Positive correlation coefficients were discovered for Hispanics as well as eligibility for both Congregate meals and School Breakfast.

Significant positive correlations were determined for whites and social security; Blacks and veterans' benefits; and nonwhites and veterans' benefits. A negative correlation occurred for Hispanics and Medicaid. Being Hispanic was found to be negatively correlated with receiving Medicaid.

Home ownership was positively associated with being white and negatively associated with being Black or being an American Indian. As a result of these associations, it appears that, among individuals receiving emergency food assistance, whites were more likely than Blacks or American Indians to own a home.

Age. Age could not be compared with other variables using the Pearson product-moment correlation. The mean age for this study was computed from ranges used by the individual surveys. The individual values for age for surveys were not known and, therefore, the correlation coefficients could not be computed.

Marital status. The associations between marital status and gender and marital status and ethnicity were discussed in the previous sections. Only five surveys queried respondents as to their marital status.

The small number of cases in this category and in other categories affected the significance of the results. Values of 0.99 and 1.00 correlations were probably due to some type of error such as small case size, rather than true linearity between the variables, and were discounted in the following discussion.

There were several correlations between marital status and income level as a percent of poverty. For the 100% of poverty level, positive correlations were calculated for the variables unmarried, divorced or separated, and single. The correlation coefficient for married individuals was negative. The direction of these associations remained the same for the 125% level, although the strength of each correlation was increased.

Pairing the level of education variables and marital status variables in this sample produced some interesting correlations. It appears that respondents with less than a high school diploma tended to be unmarried, although this was not the case for widowed individuals. Married individuals, in this sample, were more likely to have received formal education beyond high school.

Married individuals were more likely to be employed and, furthermore, were more likely to have full-time employment. For unmarried individuals the opposite was true. Marital status and the receipt of food stamps had several interesting significant correlations. Being married and receiving food stamps were negatively correlated. Single, divorced, or separated individuals were probably more likely to receive food stamps than married persons.

Education. Previously, correlations for educational level and gender, ethnicity, and marital status were discussed.

Significant correlations existed between the level of education achieved and employment status in this sample. The possession of a high school diploma or a GED was positively correlated with some employment. Attaining an education beyond the high school diploma was positively correlated with being employed and also with full-time employment. It appears that the higher the education level attained, the greater the likelihood of employment.

There were also significant correlations between the receipt of certain income benefits and education level. Social security retirement income was positively associated with less than a high school education. Veterans' benefits were positively associated with education beyond high school. Medicaid was associated with less than a high school education and negatively associated with education beyond high school.

Receipt of food stamps was positively associated with less than a high school diploma. The same was true of eligibility and use of Meals on Wheels. The receipt of Congregate Meals and possession of a high school diploma were positively correlated.

Interestingly enough, home ownership in this sample was positively associated with less than a high school diploma and negatively associated with education after receipt of the high school diploma.

Employment status. When examining correlations in this category, particular attention was paid to the number of cases. In previous sections, associations between employment status and gender, ethnicity, marital status, and educational level were discussed.

Significant negative associations were found for income at or below the 100% of poverty level and full-time employment, some employment, and being disabled. For no employment, however, a positive correlation existed. It appears, then, that the receipt of salaries and disability benefits may have resulted in exclusion of individuals from the 100% of poverty level.

A strong positive correlation was discovered between employment and full-time employment. This suggests that, when an individual in this particular sample group was employed, the employment was most likely full-time rather than part-time.

A positive correlation existed between food stamps usage and being disabled. There was a strong negative correlation for food stamps and full-time employment. Unemployment and Food Stamp Program participation were also positively associated. Although employed individuals may not have received food stamp benefits, they were seeking emergency food assistance.

It appears that there may have been some association between being elderly and having some employment. Significant positive correlation coefficients were calculated between "some employment" and the variables "households with elderly," "receipt of Meals on Wheels," and "social security retirement income." Owning a home and being employed part-time were positively correlated. Owning a home and being unemployed were negatively correlated. Positive correlations were found for renting and no employment, and employment and living with relatives or others. It appears that elderly homeowners may be obtaining part-time jobs in order to pay real estate taxes, utilities, and make repairs on their property. The fixed income of the elderly in this sample may not keep pace with the rising costs of home ownership.

Income. Income level and correlations with the descriptors of the categories gender, ethnicity, marital status, level of education, and employment status have been discussed in preceding sections.

Negative correlation coefficients were determined for the income level of 100% of poverty and the income source variables pension/retirement, social security retirement income, and social security disability income. A negative correlation also occurred for the association between the 125% level of poverty and the receipt of income from a pension or retirement. The receipt of these types of benefits, then, may have kept individuals out of these poverty levels.

For the categories of household size and composition and the category of income level, some interesting correlations were revealed. There was a positive association between being single and having an income of 125% of poverty level or less. This suggests that single individuals in this sample are likely to be poor. Negative correlations existed among the 100% of poverty level and households with elderly or pregnant members and households containing two adults and no children.

Income source. Previously, associations between the income source variables and, gender, ethnicity, marital status, education, employment status, and income level were discussed.

There was a positive correlation between the receipt of child support as an income source and salaries. It appears, that individuals receiving child support also were employed. A positive correlation coefficient between "household size of three" and "receipt of salary" also existed.

A positive correlation coefficient between receipt of AFDC benefits and a household size of four was revealed. A household size of four was also associated with the receipt of food stamps. This suggests that the benefits for household size of four, therefore, may be inadequate since respondents in this survey were seeking emergency food assistance.

A number of statistically significant correlation coefficients were calculated for associations with the variable AFDC. AFDC was positively correlated with the receipt of food stamps and AFDC was negatively correlated with not receiving food stamps. Furthermore, there was a positive correlation between the receipt of AFDC benefits and running out of food stamps. It can be suggested, therefore, that individuals who received AFDC benefits not only received food stamps, but also ran out of food stamps more than individuals who did not receive AFDC.

AFDC was also correlated with the receipt of Medicaid and WIC. As a result of this information, it can be suggested that when individuals were recipients of AFDC, they were also participants in a number of other benefit programs.

Indeed, it seems to have been the case that individuals in this sample were likely to use more than one benefit program. The correlation coefficient for food stamp use and the receipt of Medicaid benefits was positive. This suggests that individuals using Medicaid were also likely to be receiving food stamps. There was a positive association between the receipt of pension or retirement benefits and owning one's home.

Household size. Previously, correlations between household size and gender, ethnicity, marital status, educational level, employment status, income level, and income source were discussed.

As noted earlier, a household size of one was positively correlated with males and with nonwhites. Nonwhite males, in this sample, probably comprised a larger portion of homeless males than white males.

Positive correlation coefficients were calculated for a household size of one and non-receipt of food stamps, eligibility for Congregate meals, social security disability income, veterans' benefits, and being homeless. Negative correlations were revealed for this household size and the eligibility for and receipt of WIC benefits, participation in the School Lunch program, and the receipt of Medicaid benefits. It appears that persons who stated that they live alone were, for the most part, single males who may have been homeless, veterans , and/or disabled.

For household sizes exceeding one, some significant correlations exist. After review of the correlation coefficients, it appears that households of four persons usually consisted of single adults with children. For a household size of four, positive correlations existed between the receipt of food stamps, food stamps not lasting the entire month, receipt of WIC, School Lunch, AFDC, Medicaid and renting one's place of residence. A negative correlation existed for Congregate Meal eligibility. These correlations suggest that most households of four consisted of single women with children who rely heavily on government benefits and food assistance programs. In spite of this apparently heavy reliance on government programs, hunger was positively associated with a household size of four.

Household sizes of three and five were positively correlated with the variable "two adults with children." As a result of these findings it can be implied that these household sizes usually consisted of two adults with one or three children present.

Pregnancy and a household size of three were positively associated. In this sample, then, pregnancy occurred most often in households with three members. Also, positive associations occurred when "household size three" was paired with food stamps running out, WIC, WIC eligibility, School Lunch, and being hungry. Children in this group were not hungry. It appears that children may have been spared from hunger because of WIC and School Lunch, but inadequate food stamp allotment resulted in hunger in the adults in this household size of three.

In households containing five members, WIC and School Lunch were positively correlated and these associations were stronger than those for household sizes of three and four. A negative association was revealed for household size of five and being homeless. This household size was correlated with children living in the household and receipt of benefits to aid in feeding their children.

When household size increased to six or more, a number of interesting associations were noted. Significant associations between this household size and participation in Head Start meals and Medicaid occurred. The significant correlations that existed between the variables WIC, School Lunch and Medicaid and smaller household size disappeared. This was probably caused by small case numbers for the variable "household size of six or more." This reduced the opportunity to examine the relationship between the proportion for household size of six or more and other pertinent variables.

Household composition. Significant associations between household composition and gender, ethnicity, marital status, educational level, employment status, income level, income source, and household size have been discussed in previous sections.

As noted in the previous section, single adults with no children were negatively associated with the receipt of food stamps, WIC, School Lunch, and Medicaid. A positive correlation occurred for the receipt of veterans' benefits and not having cooking facilities. Based on these findings it can be suggested that these individuals were homeless.

A strong positive association was revealed when the variable "single with children" was paired with the variable "receives food stamps." A strong positive correlation also existed between single adult households with children and food stamps running out before months' end. This reaffirms associations noted in the previous section. Households in which children were present received food stamps and stamps did not last the entire month. Single adult households were not receiving food stamps. Households in which a single adult cares for a child or children also showed positive correlations with renting, and the receipt of WIC, School Lunch, and AFDC. This corroborates earlier correlations. Households in which children were present tended, according to the significant positive correlations, to be users of Head Start, AFDC, and Medicaid.

For those households in which elderly members resided, there was a positive correlation between receipt of Meals on Wheels and Congregate Meals. This suggests good use of elderly nutrition programs by the elderly members of this sample. The fact that they were still seeking emergency food assistance should be the topic of further investigation. The variable "households with elderly" also was positively associated with social security disability income and home ownership.

Households consisting of two adults, with children and home ownership were also positively correlated. This household composition also produced positive correlations with the variables WIC and WIC eligibility, School Lunch, and Medicaid. Negative correlation coefficients were calculated for no cooking facilities. It can be implied, therefore, that members of this type of household composition did not tend to be homeless.

Special dietary needs. Previously, correlations between special dietary needs and gender, ethnicity, marital status, education, employment status, income level, income source, household size, and household composition were discussed.

Very small case numbers for these descriptor variables limit the scope of this discussion. Only a few pairings occurred in which case size was large enough to permit discussion of the significant correlations.

Pregnancy and the receipt of general assistance were positively correlated. A positive association also existed for the variables "pregnancy" and "hunger." This indicates that hunger may have existed in this at-risk group.

Food stamp participation. Associations between food stamp descriptor variables and variables for gender, ethnicity, marital status, education, employment status, income level, income source, household size, household composition, and special dietary needs have been examined in previous sections.

Significant positive correlations were revealed for the receipt of food stamps and participation in School Breakfast, AFDC, and Medicaid. There was also a positive association between renting a dwelling and the receipt of food stamps. Furthermore, the correlation coefficient for food stamp receipt and running out of food stamps indicates that most recipients of food stamps in this sample also reported that food stamps did not last until the end of the month. Positive associations were also recorded between food stamps running out before the end of the month and receipt of WIC benefits, head start meals, AFDC, and Medicaid.

Participation in other government food assistance programs. In previous sections, discussion has included significant correlation coefficients for other government food assistance programs and gender, ethnicity, marital status, educational level, employment status, income level, income source, household size, household composition, special dietary needs, and participation in the food stamp program.

Positive correlations existed between the variable "receipt of Meals on Wheels" and participation in Congregate Meals Program, receipt of surplus commodities, social security disability income, and owning a dwelling. Positive associations were revealed between the receipt of social security disability income and both participation in congregate meal programs and receipt of surplus commodities. This indicates that elderly and/or disabled individuals were receiving food aid from a number of different sources.

Households that participated in the WIC program also benefitted from School Lunch, AFDC and Medicaid. A significant positive correlation coefficient was revealed for the paired variables "School Breakfast" and "Medicaid." School Lunch and Medicaid were also positively correlated. School breakfast and School Lunch were also negatively associated with no cooking facilities. This implies that recipients of School Lunch and School Breakfast were from impoverished households, but they were not homeless.

Participation in government assistance programs. In previous sections the correlations between "government assistance programs" variables and gender, ethnicity, marital status, educational level, employment status, income level, income source, household size, household composition, special dietary needs, participation in the food stamp program, and participation in other government food assistance programs were discussed.

A number of interesting associations existed among the variables for government assistance programs themselves. A significant positive correlation coefficient was calculated when the variables "AFDC" and "Medicaid" were paired with one another. A positive association was revealed between general assistance and social security disability income.

This suggests that users of benefits sometimes received benefits from more than one source.

Being a recipient of AFDC benefits and renting a dwelling were positively correlated. Ownership of the primary place of residence and social security retirement income were positively associated. It appears that, among individuals receiving emergency food assistance, the elderly owned their own homes and single mothers with children were tenants.

Living conditions. Previously, "living conditions" variable and all other descriptor variables were discussed.

A positive association was observed for being homeless and not having cooking facilities. This finding was expected since homeless people do not have access to cooking facilities. A positive correlation between the category "live other" and being homeless was calculated. It appears that the "live other" category may represent people living on the street.

Geographic location and type of locale. Differences between variables at geographic locations could not be determined due to the fact that certain geographic regions were disproportionately represented in this study. Table 3 depicts the distribution of the 27 studies by geographic region.

Type of locale. Table 3 depicts the distribution of cases by type of locale. Analysis of differences between variables based on type of locale could not be performed because of insufficient case numbers.

Summary. Based on the results of the analysis, significant Pearson product-moment correlations for a number of important interactions were found to occur among descriptor variables in the data set. Implications have been drawn from these correlation coefficients. It should be recognized, however, that where type I error has occurred, the explanation of the correlations is invalid.

A variety of interesting demographic data was obtained by examining the correlation coefficients. Males, in this sample, were predominantly nonwhite, whereas females tended to be white. The majority of Hispanic respondents were males and Hispanic participants were more likely to be married. Females were more likely than males to be poorly educated and single, divorced, or separated. Unmarried individuals were more likely to be living in poverty than married persons and married individuals were more likely to be employed.

In this sample men were more educated than women. The most educated individuals were Hispanic. Education beyond high school was associated with full-time employment. Less than high school education was associated with the receipt of food stamps, disability, Meals on Wheels and the receipt of Medicaid. Failure to achieve a high school diploma resulted in a greater probability of the receipt of government benefit programs.

When an individual was employed, employment was likely to be full-time rather than part-time. Asians were likely to be employed. Among Hispanics, employment was most likely to be full-time. Employment was positively correlated with education. Possession of a high school diploma or GED was positively associated with some employment. Food stamps were usually received by the unemployed rather than the employed.

The receipt of salaries may have resulted in the exclusion of individuals from the 100% of poverty level. For the income level category there was some indication that social security retirement income and social security disability income may have kept people out of poverty. Single individuals in the sample were likely to be poor, whereas, elderly and pregnant women were not as impoverished as singles.

Food stamp use was coupled with the use of other benefit programs such as AFDC, Medicaid, and supplemental social security. Food stamp use was correlated with females, being unmarried, and individuals possessing less than a high school education. Individuals in a household of four, particularly those with a household composition of single adult/with children, were likely to use food stamps. The receipt of food stamps was also associated with School Breakfast participation. Unemployment, part-time employment and/or being disabled were all correlated with food stamp usage. Hispanics and American Indians were less likely than other groups to use food stamps. A strong association existed between individuals who reported the receipt of food stamps and those who reported running out of food stamps prior to the end of the month. This was particularly true in households with children.

Variables in the "living conditions" category were associated with a variety of interesting variables. The homeless in this sample were likely to be males. They did not receive food stamps or a variety of other benefits. Part-time employment was correlated with home ownership. Renting was associated with no employment. Home ownership was most likely to occur in women, in whites, and/or individuals with less than a high school education.

Individuals who received one government assistance benefit frequently received other forms of government assistance. The receipt of AFDC was associated with the receipt of food stamps, Medicaid, and WIC. Households participating in WIC were likely to be the recipients of School Lunch, AFDC, and Medicaid.

Single adult households with children were headed by women. A wide variety of benefit programs including WIC, AFDC, and School Lunch were received. Respondents in this group reported the receipt of food stamps, but they also reported that the supply of stamps was inadequate. These households usually consisted of four individuals and rented their place of residence.

In households where children were present, the survey respondent was likely to be white, receiving Medicaid benefits, AFDC, and were not homeless. When School Lunch was received, the household may also have received WIC, Medicaid, AFDC, and child support.

The elderly in this sample tended to be recipients of Meals on Wheels and Congregate meals. Elderly respondents may also have been heavy users of surplus commodities. The elderly received income from social security disability income, social security retirement income, and/or pension retirement. In addition, a high correlation between the variable "some employment" and the elderly, indicates that the elderly also relied upon income from salaries.

V

Evaluation of the Methodology

The application of meta-analysis for the examination of survey research is a relatively new use of this methodology. In this particular study, meta-analysis was used to provide a framework for the investigation of a complicated public health problem. The first section of this chapter is devoted to a discussion of the problems and limitations of this particular study. In the second section of this chapter, suggestions, based on experiences of this inquiry, are made for guidelines that will enhance the outcome of future meta-analytic investigations of survey research.

PROBLEMS AND LIMITATIONS

A study of this type may be plagued with certain inherent threats to its reliability and validity. The following is a discussion of possible problems and limitations that may detract from the results of the study. Where appropriate, a discussion of attempts to correct these problems is included in this section.

As noted previously, an essential feature of meta-analysis is the successful discovery of all studies. In spite of the fact that exhaustive searches were undertaken, it should be recognized that these efforts may not have revealed all existing hunger surveys from the time frame of interest.

Since meta-analysis uses results from other studies, the addition of unreliable or invalid studies compounds problems at the time of the final analysis. Weighting of the studies was, therefore, undertaken in order to dampen the effect of numbers from poor studies.

Proportions were used in the statistical analysis because primary data, in this study, could not be obtained for all surveys. Proportions were computed for the proportion of each variable based on the number of cases for that particular variable. Error can also be introduced by the researcher when proportions are inaccurately computed from the original data or when the investigators failed to properly report the original data. Inaccurate computation of the proportions will cause misinterpretation by the meta-analyst and can subsequently result in incorrect data being added to the statistical profile. It should also be noted that the researcher cannot be assured that the data collectors from each individual survey properly interpreted or gathered the data. The weighting system employed in this study is an attempt to give greater credit to studies that followed proper survey methodology in both the collection and interpretation of data.

Only two surveys used in the statistical portion of this study employed true random sampling techniques. These studies received higher weighting scores as a result of their use of random sampling procedures. Random sampling is the superior method of sample selection because it provides a sample that is representative of the population.

Another type of error may have occurred as a result of misinterpretation of the questions by the respondent, the interviewer, or this researcher. This problem is recognized and corrected for by the use of the weighting scale. Surveys that used ambiguous questions, for example, received less weighting than surveys that used clear questions.

It should be noted that a large number of open cells existed in this study due to the fact that not all of the 17 categories of questions were addressed by each survey. Table 4 is used to depict, not only the individual surveys that contained questions in each of the 17 coding categories, but also the totals for the number of surveys that included questions in each category.

Sampling error also occurred because not all discovered surveys could be included in the statistical analysis. Studies with large defects in study design were omitted as well as studies that did not address questions addressed in the 17 categories. Exclusion of these surveys caused a bias and resulted, for example, in certain regions of the country, locales, and assistance sites being over-represented or under-represented.

The numerical analysis in this study is based only on characteristics of individuals who were actively seeking food at emergency assistance sights. This analysis does not include individuals who may have required

Table 4: Questions Utilized in Surveys (cases) by Coding Category Descriptors

Survey	1	2	3	4	5	6	7	8	9
DESCRIPTORS									
Gender	x	x	x	x	x	x	x	x	x
Ethnicity	x	x	x			x	x	x	x
Age	x	x	x	x	x	x	x	x	x
Marital Status		x			x				
Education		x			x	x	x	x	x
Employment Status		x	x		x	x	x	x	x
Income Level	x	x	x		x	x	x	x	x
Income Source	x		x		x	x	x	x	x
Household Size	x	x	x	x	x	x	x	x	x
Household Composition	x		x		x	x	x	x	x
Special Diet			x		x	x	x	x	x
Food Stamps	x	x	x	x	x	x	x	x	x
Government Food Assistance			x		x	x	x	x	x
Other Government Assistance	x		x		x	x	x	x	x
Hunger Perception	x	x	x	x	x	x	x	x	x
Living Conditions	x			x	x	x	x	x	x

Table 4: Questions Utilized in Surveys (cases) by Coding Category Descriptors

Survey	10	11	12	13	14	15	16	17	18
DESCRIPTORS									
Gender	x	x	x	x	x	x			x
Ethnicity	x	x	x	x		x	x		x
Age	x	x	x	x	x	x		x	x
Marital Status				x		x			
Education	x	x	x	x		x		x	
Employment Status	x	x	x	x				x	x
Income Level	x	x	x	x			x		x
Income Source	x	x	x	x	x	x		x	x
Household Size	x	x	x	x				x	
Household Composition	x	x	x	x				x	
Special Diet					x		x		x
Food Stamps	x	x	x	x	x	x	x	x	x
Government Food Assistance	x	x	x				x		x
Other Government Assistance	x	x	x	x	x	x		x	x
Hunger Perception	x	x	x		x	x	x		x
Living Conditions	x	x	x		x	x			

Table 4: Questions Utilized in Surveys (cases) by Coding Category Descriptors

Survey	19	20	21	22	23	24	25	26	27	Total
DESCRIPTORS										
Gender				x	x	x	x			20
Ethnicity	x			x		x	x	x		19
Age			x	x	x	x	x	x	x	24
Marital Status				x						5
Education				x	x					14
Employment Status		x		x	x	x	x			18
Income Level	x	x		x		x	x			19
Income Source	x	x		x	x	x	x	x	x	23
Household Size		x				x	x			17
Household Composition		x	x			x	x			16
Special Diet					x	x	x			12
Food Stamps	x	x	x	x	x	x	x	x	x	27
Government Food Assistance	x			x				x	x	15
Other Government Assistance		x		x	x	x	x			20
Hunger Perception						x	x			18
Living Conditions	x	x	x	x	x		x	x	x	20

emergency food assistance, but did not seek this type of aid; individuals who did not have access to these facilities; and individuals who did not participate in the surveys.

META-ANALYSIS AND SURVEY RESEARCH

It is imperative that the researchers strictly adhere to the six rules for successful administration of the meta-analysis which were delineated in Chapter Three. These six steps are: specification of the research question(s); delineation of the research domain; review of the literature; assessment of the literature; analysis of the sample; and summary of the analysis. Rigorous conformity to these guidelines should be the case in any meta-analytic investigation, but it is of definite merit when examining surveys. Surveys, by their very nature, have a subjective component, and strict obedience to the principles of research conduct promises less possibility that bias will be introduced by the meta-analyst. The following paragraphs provide suggestions for success in meta-analysis of surveys.

Specification of the Research Question(s)

Specification of the research question is a vital element in a successful meta-analysis of surveys. Lack of this central focus could lead to the introduction of subjectivity by the researcher. Surveys provide a wealth of information about a host of societal trends. Investigators who fail to specify a research question may be pulled in a variety of directions and, in turn, may focus on information that is tangential to the main issues of the study.

Delineation of the Research Domain

Delineation of the research domain is crucial in all meta-analyses, but carries significant weight in investigations of surveys. Again, this is an area where subjectivity can occur. The researcher must take particular pains to insure that the research domain encompasses the entirety of the research question. Furthermore, the selection of the time frame is critically important in meta-analysis. Investigators should pay close attention to the time frame of the survey, since survey publication dates are far different from the actual date of the survey. This becomes particularly important later in the analysis when trends are assessed.

Review of the Literature

The literature review is yet another area in which subjectivity can occur. The review of the literature must accurately investigate the entire research domain. The importance of the use of published and unpublished data is the subject of debate among meta-analysts. This debate has particular impact when examining surveys, since many surveys are not published. Surveys undertaken for a specific interest group are not available to an audience beyond this target group. Even many government surveys are not published and distributed. In the case of some larger government surveys, a portion of the data tapes may be extracted, analyzed, and then published in a refereed journal.

Unpublished surveys provide a large portion of the data available for analysis. Unique and unconventional methods may be required in order to ferret out unpublished surveys. The investigator must be willing to explore new avenues for the collection of the surveys. In this study, for instance, it was discovered that one anti-hunger group collected a large number of hunger surveys. The researcher visited this agency and collected surveys from their extensive files.

A list of agencies and individuals of importance to the anti-hunger movement was developed from this study. Letters were sent to members of this list as well as the chief health officer of each state. The purpose of this letter was to inquire as to whether or not the individual had performed any surveys or knew of surveys performed in the time frame of interest. These two strategies of collection proved valuable avenues in the discovery of hunger surveys. Similar methods could be adopted by researchers examining surveys in other topic areas.

The investigator must also go beyond traditional database searches. Newspapers and magazines provide timely information about unpublished surveys. Prior to the search, a reference librarian in the appropriate field of study should be consulted. Librarians are privy to the latest databases and the inclusion of a reference librarian in the early stages will ultimately save research time and prevent the omission of valuable surveys.

After discovering the existence and location of completed surveys, every attempt should be made to obtain the original data. This is particularly important for survey research because the information collected in a survey is unique to the sampled population at that particular point in time.

Assessment of the Literature

After gathering all surveys that meet selection criteria, the meta-analyst must begin sifting through the surveys. Reasons for survey exclusion should be logged and the investigator should develop a chart of inclusion criteria in order to present survey observations in an organized, readable fashion.

Establishing question categories is also a critical portion of studying survey research. Since surveys rarely use the same form for specific questions, establishing guidelines for question categories is a difficult and sensitive process. Questions must be removed from consideration if the intent of a question cannot be determined. However, sometimes questions that are removed from consideration can provide useful information in the qualitative analysis portion of the study.

Establishing these question categories may also prove useful in the analysis portion of the study since these question categories themselves reveal important areas of investigation for future survey efforts. These categories may provide the questions for future surveys on the topic.

Finally, developing a method for weighting the surveys is crucial to a successful outcome in this type of meta-analysis. Surveys possess a variety of areas in which biases can be introduced. An appropriate weighting system can assist in attenuating the results of poorly designed, poorly implemented, and/or poorly reported surveys. More than one researcher should evaluate the surveys in order to insure less bias. Ideally, more than one researcher should also determine the evaluation criteria.

Analysis of the Sample

A statistician should be consulted for the statistical portion of the analysis. The statistician may recommend alternative ways of viewing the data. In this particular analysis, for instance, scatterplots were recommended as a way of finding possible trends in interest areas that possessed small cell sizes.

Summary of the Analysis

The summary of the analysis is a very important and frequently neglected area of studies. This summary should include a discussion of general trends related to both the qualitative and quantitative portions of the study. The baseline information produced by the quantitative analysis is an important resource for making comments about the subject of the survey. The meta-analyst is in a unique position to recognize trends because of the extensive database and thoroughness of the investigation. Even the survey questions and the format of the surveys may reflect changes in research interests and policy focus over a given period of time.

Summary

Meta-analysis can provide a useful framework for the study of survey research. When the six guidelines for the conduct of meta-analyses are strictly adhered to the outcome of the research is far more valid. In order to add further objectivity to this process, more than one researcher should be involved in the process. Bias can be introduced in any of the six steps of the analysis. Although this effect is attenuated by the weighting system, less bias would be introduced if more than one researcher analyzes the surveys.

Meta-analysis of a set of surveys in a specific topic area may result in suggestions for improvement in the construction, administration, analysis, and reporting of future surveys. This type of information can save time and money for future researchers. In addition, adherence to these guidelines can prevent error which may dramatically affect the results of the meta-analysis.

Meta-analysis is a valuable tool for policy planning because it gleans and collects valuable information that is sprinkled across the literature. Information culled from the meta-analysis of survey research is particularly useful to policy makers because surveys provide a unique view of human nature and of the development of societal trends. This information can be used to recommend actions for policy makers.

VI

Policy Implications

In this chapter the qualitative and quantitative analyses as well as the information discovered in the literature review are used to discuss the policy implications of this research.

GOVERNMENT FOOD ASSISTANCE POLICY IN THE 1980S

Federal food assistance programs in the United States are specifically designed to alleviate hunger, therefore, the reemergence of the hunger problem during the 1980s infers a failure of these programs. Hunger in the United States was virtually eliminated in the latter part of the 1970s and food assistance programs have been largely credited with this reduction in the number of hungry people. In the 1980s, however, a sharp rise in the number of individuals seeking emergency food assistance was observed. An economic recession early in the decade led to an increase in the number of people who were eligible for government food assistance. A series of budget reductions to these food assistance programs restricted program usage. In addition to the profound and immediate effects of these economic alterations, this study found a series of existing problems related to the government food assistance programs that ultimately led to the escalation of emergency food assistance requests.

Government food assistance policies of the 1980s created a climate which allowed for the weaknesses in the federal food assistance structure to be revealed. The failure to develop techniques for measurement and a system for monitoring and surveillance of the hungry created an excessive reliance on anecdotal reports. The resulting information void virtually abrogated the authority of Congress to respond in an appropriate fashion. As the economy changed, limitations and problems in existing food assistance programs were exacerbated by a rapid growth in eligible participants. The government had failed to develop food assistance programs that were responsive to shifts in eligibility rates, benefit needs, and participation rates. Finally, an integrated umbrella of nutrition policy which would have provided a thread of continuity to the fragmented food assistance programs did not exist.

Failure to Develop Measurement Techniques

The government failed to develop techniques for the collection of information about individuals experiencing hunger or those who are at-risk for hunger. Furthermore, the government and researchers failed to clearly define what is meant by hunger among members of the United States population. A universally acceptable definition would aid in the data collection process and clear the ground for debate.

Hunger research during the decade was largely confined to state reports and to surveys done by private agencies. Study results were usually shared with a small target audience such as the members of a church board of directors. Because of this type of reporting, policy makers usually had no indication of the results of these studies.

These studies were plagued by a litany of problems including: poor survey design; poor methodological procedures; lack of uniformity of question areas; and lack of uniform variable assessment. Studies lacked geographic representation and standards for timeliness in data collection. Personnel involved in surveys were frequently untrained in survey administration techniques, data analysis, and result reporting. Although the sophistication of the surveys increased as the decade progressed, overall the surveys were poorly designed.

Failure to Inaugurate Surveillance and Monitoring

The U.S. government's lack of commitment to the development of a system for the timely investigation and reporting of information pertaining to at-risk groups contributed to the hunger problem of the decade. The way in which the government sought to examine the hunger problem in the 1980s was through existing methods of monitoring and surveillance.

During the decade, government relied on the nutritional measurements obtained by NHANES and food consumption data discovered by the NFCS to provide statistics about hungry people. NHANES was conducted only twice in the 1980s and the results were not reported in a timely fashion. This rendered this information of little use to hunger researchers, policy makers, and government officials who were faced with dynamic and swift changes in the number of eligible individuals.

Failure to inaugurate successful monitoring and surveillance contributed to the problem of uninformed policy decisions. This lack of data resulted in an unbalanced reliance on anecdotal information. Congressional battles for the establishment of a national nutrition monitoring system characterized the decade.

Failure to Identify the Characteristics of the Clientele

This lack of measurement, monitoring, and surveillance resulted in predictable difficulties. Knowledge of the characteristics and changing needs of a client-base are crucial issues in successful program planning. The quantitative portion of the meta-analysis indicated some relationships between the various characteristics of individuals who sought emergency food assistance and received aid from government food assistance programs. These relationships will be examined in the following paragraphs.

Certain groups are at-risk for hunger and many of our efforts from the standpoint of subsidized food assistance programs have been focused on these groups. It was revealed in the quantitative portion of the meta-analysis that groups that were participating in government food assistance programs were still seeking emergency food assistance. This is troubling since these programs were designed to alleviate hunger within these groups.

The marked increase in the number of individuals queuing up at soup kitchens and food banks demonstrates that some individuals were unable to obtain food assistance through normal government channels. Information from this study provides some indication of these problems for specific food assistance program recipients. The failure of these food assistance programs can be linked to eligibility requirements, benefit levels, and participation rates. The following is a brief discussion of conclusions drawn from an examination of the data analysis.

Surplus commodities. Surplus commodities were received by the impoverished elderly and the disabled. There was some indication that individuals eligible for Congregate Meals and those who received Congregate Meals used food stamps. Surplus commodities also were obtained by some individuals who received Meals on Wheels. This may indicate that the Meals on Wheels program did not provide adequate food for daily needs and that the elderly used surplus commodities to supplement the food received from Meals on Wheels. The elderly, in this sample, may not have possessed adequate income to meet basic living expenses.

Food stamps. The attendance of individuals at emergency food assistance sites who also reported the use of food stamps (48%) indicates that food stamp allotment for these individuals was too low. Although food stamps were effective in eliminating hunger among household members, 71% of food stamp recipients indicated that their food stamps ran out before month's end. When their food stamps ran out, respondents indicated that hunger returned to the household. Individuals using food stamps were frequently forced to rely on other food assistance programs. Food stamp use was associated with the use of WIC, School Breakfast, School Lunch, Congregate Meals, and Meals on Wheels. During the decade, food stamp allotment was insufficient to totally eliminate hunger among a great proportion of recipients.

Participation in other government assistance programs. Participation in food assistance programs was usually coupled with participation in some other type of government assistance program such as AFDC or Social Security Disability Income. Government assistance programs, then, failed to meet client needs and individuals were forced to use government food assistance programs. In addition, respondents in this study frequently used more than one type of government aid such as AFDC and Medicaid.

This indicates that benefit levels for these programs were too low to provide for the basic needs of the recipients.

Child nutrition programs. Large discrepancies in the number of individuals who were eligible for School Breakfast and the number of individuals participating in the program were reported in this study. The same type of inconsistency was found in the case of School Lunch, although the disparity between eligibility and participation was not as pronounced. Barriers to participation in School Breakfast programs existed at the state and local levels primarily because School Breakfast was not always offered by school districts. Individuals who reported eligibility for School Lunch, also stated that they were hungry. School Breakfast has a clear role in alleviating hunger and should have been available to all eligible children.

Elderly nutrition programs. Results from this study suggest that the elderly nutrition programs (i.e., Congregate Meals and Meals on Wheels) were well-used by the eligible population. The elderly, however, were still visiting emergency food assistance sites. This indicates that benefit levels were too low in relation to demand for food.

WIC. Correlations suggested that there were individuals eligible for WIC who were not participating in the program. In fact, the study indicated generally low participation rates. Yet, a negative correlation between WIC use and hunger suggested that hunger was alleviated among WIC participants. The study also revealed that, frequently, when WIC was used so were food stamps. This suggests that WIC benefit levels were low in relation to demand for food or that individuals in the WIC household relied on food stamps in order to purchase food.

Failure to Develop a National Nutrition Policy

At the root of this failure by the U.S. government to effectively define, measure, monitor, and combat hunger in the United States in the 1980s was the lack of a national nutrition policy. A strong central nutrition policy would include a strategy for the control and eradication of hunger through the use of the regulatory powers of government. Such a national nutrition policy would provide a continuity and design of purpose that would have served to provide the appropriate climate for mitigating the numbers of hungry people.

Furthermore, such a policy would provide a framework for food assistance programs. The assistance programs would be equipped with direction and continuity. The present piecemeal approach to food assistance would be replaced with a central focus for the currently fragmented efforts and would exist as just one cog in the nutrition plan for the nation.

FUTURE GOVERNMENT FOOD ASSISTANCE POLICY

Information from this study can be used in three ways to aid in future policy decisions pertaining to U.S. food assistance policy. These three mechanisms are addressed in the following sections of this chapter. First, information from this study can be used to enhance future hunger measurement, monitoring, and surveillance efforts. Suggestions regarding survey design, conduct, and reporting will be made. Second, recommendations for short term improvements to existing food assistance programs will be addressed. Third, long term issues related to the hunger problem such as housing, health care, and education will be discussed.

Measurement, Monitoring, and Surveillance

Food assistance policy makers in the 1980s were hamstrung by a lack of data that had been collected in a reliable and timely fashion. Information collected in NHANES took a protracted period of time to be disseminated. This failure by the U.S. government to develop measurement, monitoring, and surveillance techniques hobbled the efforts of hunger researchers.

Baseline data is an important component in this type of research. Information from this sample should be used to make comments about future measurement of the problem. The Coded Categorical Variables developed for this study are based on careful examination of hunger studies conducted in the 1980s. Core questions derived from this examination are represented in the seventeen coding categorical variables described in Chapter Three. All questions should be asked in a uniform fashion using U. S. Bureau of the Census or U.S. Bureau of Labor Statistics guidelines. This type of uniformity will insure comparability of the data between hunger surveys as well as with other general population surveys. Future surveys should include more questions regarding accessibility and eligibility for the various food assistance programs. An individual's perception of his or her own hunger is a critical component of this research. A surprising number of surveys, however, did not ask participants if they were hungry. This may, in part, be due to the lack of agreement with regard to a definition of hunger.

The passage of the National Nutrition Monitoring and Related Research Act of 1990 could change the way in which we examine and conquer hunger in the United States. This law mandates that at-risk populations be monitored for their nutritional status. This legislation could have a pronounced impact on hunger surveillance and, therefore, sufficient funding should be appropriated for this law. An elected body should monitor the collection process and formulate policy that is based on this data. In addition, these elected officials should provide continuity between food assistance programs and provide a public forum in which citizens can address hunger issues. The House of Representatives Select Committee on Hunger can provide this type of guidance.

Food Assistance Programs

Data from this study can aid in constructing questions targeted at specific aspects of food assistance program policy in the U.S. Client characteristics revealed in the quantitative analysis section of this study define areas of food assistance programs that deserve intense scrutiny. First, access barriers, eligibility determinants, participation rates, and benefit levels for virtually all food assistance programs should be examined. Second, the apparent insensitivity of food assistance programs to detect and react to economic changes deserves further attention. Third, the fragmented, piecemeal nature of food assistance in the U.S. may suggest the necessity for a complete overhaul of government food assistance policy.

In this study all programs, except for surplus commodities, showed higher eligibility rates than participation rates. The number of individuals eligible for food stamps far exceeded the number who were actually receiving food stamps. This disparity also existed between participation and eligibility for the School Lunch Program and School Breakfast participation lagged behind School Lunch participation. School Breakfast is unavailable in many school districts and this may account for these low participation rates. Studies have shown that children learn better when they are fed. School officials, policy makers, and Congress should work together to eliminate barriers to participation in School Lunch and School Breakfast. The higher rates of eligibility than participation that existed in the WIC program are also troubling. WIC helps to meet the nutritional needs of at-risk populations and as such is an important prevention program. For the elderly, another at-risk population, there were more eligible individuals than participants for elderly nutrition programs. Again, this may indicate access problems such as transportation, program availability, and complicated application procedures.

The apparent disparity between eligibility and participation rates in many of the food assistance programs indicates problems with the programs. Policy makers should examine possible barriers to participation such as program availability and administrational quagmires. For at-risk populations such as the elderly, pregnant females, and children, this lack of participation may have significant health repercussions and also economic ramifications associated with the cost of treating illness and hospitalization.

Apparent insufficiencies in food stamp benefits requires further examination. Many recipients of food stamps, in this study, reported that their food stamps ran out before the end of the month. In addition, individuals whose food stamps ran out reported that they were hungry. If this is indeed the case, benefit levels may need to be increased so that the stamps will last the entire month.

This study revealed that in many cases more than one type of food assistance was being used by an individual or family. The heavy reliance on surplus commodities by recipients of elderly nutrition programs is an area that demands further investigation. The use of both surplus commodities and elderly nutrition programs by individuals in this sample indicates that the elderly nutrition programs were inadequate in meeting the needs of this population. When surplus commodities were unavailable, the elderly may have gone without food in order to pay for such necessities as utilities and pharmaceuticals. Many of the food assistance program participants also reported reliance on other forms of government assistance.

As the economy worsened in the early 1980s, the gaps between participation and eligibility widened and benefit levels were insufficient to meet food needs. A system which is sensitive to economic fluctuations needs to be developed. In such a system, application procedures could be accelerated and necessary appropriations could be swiftly funneled into the appropriate food assistance programs. In this manner, hungry individuals could be aided more quickly. The formula for benefit level calculation should be reevaluated. Household size, the number of children and adults residing within a household, should not be the only factor. The age of each child should be an important factor in the calculation of benefit levels. The fact that teenagers consume as much, if not more, food than an adult should be recognized in this equation.

Low participation rates, low benefit levels, and reliance on more than one food assistance program indicates wide scale problems with the system of food assistance in the United States. Food assistance in the U.S. is fragmented and under the auspices of several different agencies. Food assistance programs are not controlled and monitored by any one group. There is a heavy reliance on the private sector to compensate for the inadequacies of the government programs. Extensive restructuring of government food assistance programs must occur in order to effectively eradicate hunger among U.S. citizens. Changes must include the development of food assistance programs that are far more sensitive to fluctuating needs and programs should be controlled by one government agency.

Factors Related to Hunger

Not all the problems with hunger in the U.S. can be blamed on failed food assistance programs. Hunger, in this study, was linked to a wide variety of social welfare problems including: poverty, employment, housing, education, household composition, and health care. Understanding the connection between these factors and hunger is critical to the amelioration of the hunger problem in the U.S.

Poverty. Poverty, which has been linked to a variety of health issues such as underinsurance and poor health status, emerged in this study as an indicator of hunger. Individuals living at the poverty level comprised 75% of participants. The number of households reporting incomes at 125% of poverty level was 83%. Clearly, most individuals seeking emergency food assistance were impoverished. The level of income also had an effect on hunger variables in this study. As income decreased, reported hunger increased. Poverty, then, is strongly associated with hunger and as such must be addressed as an issue in food assistance debates.

The number of individuals living in poverty as well as the number of children living in poverty grew in the 1980s. This led to an inevitable increase in the number of individuals at risk of hunger. Children under age five are not served by School Lunch and School Breakfast programs and may also not enjoy the benefits of Headstart feeding programs. Hunger in the early years is associated with impaired growth and development and increased disease risk. The long term physiologic, social, and economic costs of hunger in children may exceed the short term financial cost of feeding them.

How we will deal with impoverished people in terms of alleviating hunger should be the focus of national debate. What is clear is that immediate, short term changes in food assistance must be inaugurated in order to stem the inevitable growth in hungry people brought about by economic recessions. In the long run, however, issues of the alleviation of poverty must be considered. Income supplements, jobs, and job training are issues in the hunger debate for they impact on one of the root causes of hunger — poverty.

Employment. In the area of employment three important findings merit further consideration. First, individuals who held full-time employment appeared at emergency food assistance sites. Second, part-time employment may initiate financial difficulties. Third, a large proportion of the females in this sample were unemployed.

It appears that full-time employment alone does not necessarily preclude dependence on emergency food assistance within a household. Perhaps the current minimum wage is too low to support a decent minimum of nutrition. The nature of the minimum wage structure in the U.S. demands further analysis. An individual living in rural Arkansas, for example, will have a far different use of wages than will an individual who resides in New York City. Housing in New York City consumes a larger portion of earnings than housing in Arkansas. This results in less money with which to buy food. Disparities exist between different regions of the country for not only housing costs, but also utility, transportation, child care, health care, and clothing costs. An individual with a full-time, minimum wage job may not qualify for food stamps. Yet this same individual cannot afford to buy food because of rent, utility, health care, and clothing expenditures. This suggests that minimum wages set by economic zones or regions would be a more equitable solution.

Part-time employment presents another set of difficulties. Although the employment itself creates useable income for a household, it is an inferior form of employment. Health care insurance, retirement wages, and disability stipends are benefits that are all linked to full-time employment. In addition, increased income from part-time employment may move the household income level out of the range of certain food assistance programs. The individual who accepts part-time employment may actually be financially penalized if he or she is forced to pay health insurance and experiences benefit losses because of the receipt of income. This type of discrimination creates a climate in which individuals are reticent to seek part-time employment.

A large portion of the unemployed in this sample were women. Women are typically the caretakers of small children and are frequently unable to work because of difficulties in obtaining and paying for child care. The U.S. lacks a strong child care system and an employment environment that favor working mothers. Women are also more likely than men to leave their employment to care for an ill parent. Because the U.S. does not have family leave legislation, this means that frequently women must give up their employment and along with it, their health insurance and retirement income.

When women do work outside the home, they tend to earn less than men. Many important benefits are received by the full-time employed. These unemployed women have no health care insurance, disability insurance, or retirement wages. Divorced women do not qualify to receive their husband's retirement wages. Divorced women with children are not very successful in collecting child support unless the father is an employee of the government or a member of the military. Clearly, the government should support child care legislation, wage equity for women, and develop stronger enforcement policies for the collection of child support payments.

Housing. Several interesting observations emerged from an investigation of housing and hungry people. First, individuals who rented were far more likely to be hungry. There are specific tax advantages to home owners and home owners build equity in their homes. This equity can provide a source of income in the event of a financial crisis. Additionally, the cost of rental property may be excessively high in certain areas of the country. Individuals who spend a greater percentage of their income on housing have less disposable income for food.

Women, in this sample, who owned a home were seeking emergency food assistance. This may imply that these women were cash poor because their assets consisted of home equity. A significant portion of these women were elderly and may have held part-time employment. It seems that elderly women in this sample were having a difficult time making ends meet. Increasing costs of home maintenance, real estate taxes, and utility bills coupled with small increases in benefits from social security have caused financial hardship for many older Americans. These bills and taxes may preclude elderly homeowners from purchasing food. The need for supplemental income resulted in some retirees resorting to part-time employment in order to pay their bills and also meet basic needs.

Education. The level of education attained by an individual, in this study, appeared to be related to hunger. Individuals with a high school diploma or better reported less hunger in the household. Individuals who did not complete a high school education were more likely to receive food stamps than their more educated counterparts. This reliance on food stamps may be brought about by unemployment or low wages which also have been linked to poor education. Lack of education may also cause difficulties in understanding food stamp application procedures.

The discovery that decreased education levels is correlated to emergency food assistance adds to the considerable body of evidence that education is an important precursor to a variety of health concerns and a number of societal ills. The noncompletion of high school and its correlation to hunger merits further investigation. Issues of job training, wages, and unemployment may be important considerations in future hunger research and food assistance policy.

Household composition. In this study, two household types emerged as likely hunger risks. Single men and single women with children stated that they were hungry. Single men who were seeking emergency food assistance tended to be homeless. These men also frequented soup kitchens and reported the receipt of veterans' benefits and disability benefits. An examination of veterans' benefit levels should be undertaken in order to ascertain their adequacy.

Women and children constitute a major risk group for the physiologic effects of hunger. The fact that single mothers and their dependent children, in this sample, were soliciting emergency food assistance is troubling. A heavy reliance on government assistance was indicated by the use of School Lunch, Medicaid, AFDC, and food stamps by the members of female-headed households. The overwhelming problem of hunger in the female-headed households, in this sample, is that these women were living in poverty. The government should initiate actions designed to reduce the number of women and children living in poverty.

Health care. In this study a large percentage of the recipients reported the receipt of Medicaid insurance. A larger percentage reported Medicare receipt. This, as noted previously, probably reflects confusion as to the correct title of the program from which they were receiving health care benefits. Based on reported income levels, however, a far greater number of individuals in this sample should have been receiving Medicaid benefits. This discrepancy between eligibility and participation may be due to access problems. Medicaid recipients may be denied care because of their payment method. A second access problem occurs in obtaining the Medicaid card. Applicants must apply in person at public aid offices and must produce documentation of finances. The procedure requires a significant amount of time and bureaucracy.

The investigation of health care costs was neglected in most of the surveys. More attention needs to be paid to the effect that health care costs may have on the ability of the household to purchase food. For instance, having an individual who requires a special diet due to diabetes may increase the food costs of the household. When economic constraints result in an inability to meet special dietary needs, existing medical problems of the individual may be exacerbated. This, in turn, may lead to increased medical costs. If the individual is a recipient of Medicare or Medicaid, the financial burden of his or her care belongs to the government and the taxpayers.

Another concern with regard to health care costs is health insurance. A lack of health insurance coupled with a major medical illness may result in a family losing everything and becoming impoverished. The expenditures associated with a disabled adult may also place a financial burden on the family. Family leave policies would protect individuals who leave their jobs for family emergencies by insuring their health coverage in their absence.

Summary

Budget reductions in federal food assistance programs coupled with an economic recession created the climate for the emergence of the hunger problems of the 1980s. The sheer magnitude of media reports, studies, and surveys regarding hunger in America intimates that hunger may have reemerged as a problem in the 1980s. The apparent existence of hunger in the U.S. during this decade suggests a failure of the very programs designed to ameliorate the problem. Food assistance programs failed during this time period for many reasons. This study determined that government failed to initiate measurement of the hungry, relied on the results of non-government sources and, then, rejected these results as methodologically unsound. An appropriate system of monitoring and surveillance that would require that data about hungry people and at-risk populations be collected and disseminated in a timely fashion did not exist. Food assistance programs did not respond well to the increasing needs of their clientele. Benefit levels were too low to provide needed food, and participation rates were too low compared to eligibility rates.

Measurement is an integral component of the formation, implementation, and evaluation stages of the policy process. Accurate data has, historically, led to more informed policy decisions. The failure by the U.S. government to successfully measure the hunger problem resulted in a lack of appropriate data for the determination of policy. Information about hunger during the decade came from a vast array of resources, but the Federal government was not a leader in the collection of the data. The lack of measurement by the federal government, caused difficulties in the policy formulation process.

The National Nutrition Monitoring and Related Research Act of 1990 mandates the collection of baseline data for groups who are at risk for hunger. The manner in which this data will be collected needs to be determined. The National Nutrition Monitoring System should examine the results of this study and the surveys conducted in the 1980s in order to establish methodological considerations and possible survey questions. A central core of questions should be developed for the study of hunger.

The fragmented nature of the federal food assistance programs should be resolved. Leadership for monitoring food assistance policy, programs, and data collection should be assumed by one group. A national nutrition policy that would recognize food assistance policy as just one component of the overall picture should be formulated and adopted.

Areas that are critically linked to hunger in the population were also examined in this study. Hunger is linked to many factors including poverty, employment, housing, education, household composition, and health care costs. Problems in these areas articulate a need for a change in the approach to the eradication of hunger. Traditionally, anti-hunger activists have lobbied for increased federal funding, expanded participation rates, and the elimination of administrative barriers for food assistance programs. While these considerations still have merit as short-term goals, the results of this study indicate that there are several long-term goals that need to be realized in order to conquer the problem of hunger in the United States. Decreasing poverty, increasing income levels, increasing education levels, and establishing universal health insurance are all necessary in order to eradicate hunger in the United States.

VII

Conclusions

The purposes of this study were to determine the characteristics of individuals who self-reported hunger, to compile correlational data with regard to these characteristics, to make suggestions for the improvement of future hunger surveys, to make suggestions for future food assistance policy decisions, and to evaluate the use of meta-analysis as a technique for the examination of survey research.

Meta-analysis was used to provide a framework for the systematic examination of hunger studies conducted in the 1980s. The quantitative results of this investigation were based upon the 27 surveys chosen for statistical analysis. The conclusions and recommendations are an outgrowth of both the qualitative and quantitative portions of the meta-analysis and the investigation of U.S. hunger policy.

FINDINGS

1. The United States government did not properly monitor the extent of hunger in the United States during the 1980s. Furthermore, the government failed to plan for the continual surveillance of the population at-risk for hunger. This lack of surveillance led to a situation in which policy was formulated in the absence of accurate data.

2. The U.S. government did not develop measurement techniques for the collection of data about hungry people. This resulted in a lack of baseline information about the characteristics of people who sought emergency food assistance.

3. The government did not keep watch over the needs of at-risk population groups. The dissolution of the Senate Select Committee on Nutrition and Human Needs is an example of this type of reduction in vigilance.

4. Programs designed to ameliorate the problem of hunger were ineffective in their purpose and this is evidenced by the large numbers of individuals seeking emergency food assistance during this time frame.

5. Evidence regarding the nature and extent of the hunger problem existed, but not in an acceptable form for a full examination of the interrelationships between factors related to hunger.

6. The Food Stamp Program did not meet the needs of the hungry in America. Only 50% of people seeking food at emergency food assistance sites were recipients of food stamps. Those receiving food stamps frequently reported running out of stamps prior to the end of the month.

7. The U.S. government did not establish a national nutrition policy which would have addressed the problem of hunger in the United States.

8. Poorly educated individuals were at greater risk for hunger in this study. This conclusion is based upon the findings from the quantitative portion of the meta-analysis that indicated a correlation between hunger and individuals who possessed less than a high school education.

9. Based on the large number of employed individuals who sought emergency food assistance, it can be concluded that employment did not necessarily prevent hunger in the 1980s.

10. A large percentage of individuals seeking emergency food assistance were single women with children.

11. The income of the elderly population, in this sample, was insufficient to meet their basic needs. Thus, these individuals were forced to seek emergency food assistance.

12. Hunger in the United States is, for the most part, a result of poverty. Most survey respondents in this sample were living below the poverty line.

13. Hunger among children in the 1980s was an unfortunate reality. One-third of individuals who answered questions about their perception of hunger, stated that their children sometimes went hungry. This is a particularly alarming statistic considering the impact of inadequate sustenance on the growth and development of children.

14. Individuals using soup kitchen facilities may have been more hungry than those at food pantries. The soup kitchen clientele may have consisted of homeless people who lacked access to cooking facilities.

15. When individuals received benefits from one government assistance program, they frequently received other forms of government assistance.

16. Methodological errors in surveys led to perceived weaknesses in data. When data was weighted, however, the effect of these errors was attenuated.

17. Meta-analysis was an appropriate framework for the study of hunger surveys conducted in the United States in the 1980s. This framework provided a foundation for systematically evaluating the discovered hunger surveys.

RECOMMENDATIONS

1. The government of the United States should begin now to develop measurement techniques for establishing baseline information about the characteristics of hungry people. This baseline information will aid policy makers in establishing programs to alleviate hunger.

2. The government of the United States should begin a concerted effort to monitor the population at-risk for hunger. A system of continual surveillance of groups that are at-risk for hunger should be immediately inaugurated. This effort should include a method for the timely dissemination of the data.

3. The government should create a group to watch over the needs of hungry individuals or at-risk populations. A group such as The Senate Select Committee on Nutrition and Human Needs may be appropriate for this task. Such a group will create an advocacy group for people at-risk for hunger.

4. A hunger index should be developed immediately that would use existing government statistics to determine changes in the number of individuals who are at risk for hunger. The U.S. Bureau of Labor Statistics and the U.S. Bureau of the Census collect monthly statistics that include consumer prices, housing costs, health care costs, employment levels, and poverty levels. Existing food assistance programs should be modified to be more sensitive to economic fluctuations that impact upon an individual's ability to obtain food. A hunger index would serve as a barometer that would indicate changes in the number of individuals at-risk for hunger. Food assistance programs should be reconstructed to be sensitive to changes in this index.

5. Improvements in the Food Stamp Program should be begun immediately. Benefit, participation, and eligibility levels should be examined. Adequate allotment of benefits will mitigate the likelihood of running out of stamps prior to the end of the month. An improved Food Stamp Program will also be more sensitive to changes in the economy which may affect the number of people seeking food stamps.

6. A national nutrition policy should be formulated that would treat the eradication of hunger as an achievable goal. Such a nutrition policy would focus efforts on insuring the nutritional health of all individuals irrespective of their ability to procure food through the normal channels of trade. This type of policy would give clear direction to policy makers as to the goals and objectives of the U.S. government with respect to nutrition policy.

7. The government should treat the completion of high school as a high priority. The level of education attained by an individual continues to be linked with poor health outcomes and is, according to the results of this study, an indicator of whether or not an individual will be hungry.

8. The current minimum wage structure should be examined for its ability to support a standard quality of life. Wages should be increased by economic or enterprise zone in order to bring individuals out of the poverty level and, as a result, decrease their risk for hunger. Improvement of the wage structure will result in more equitable pay. This will result in an increase in an individual's ability to obtain the basic necessities such as food and, consequently, less reliance on the government to provide sustenance.

9. The economic and health needs of single women and their dependent children should be addressed. These individuals are at critical risk for a variety of societal and health problems. Their financial status as well as their income sources should be examined.

10. Elderly nutrition programs as well as elderly income support programs should be examined for their ability to meet the needs of the elderly.

11. The number of people in poverty in the U.S. should be reduced and long range goals for the further diminishment of poverty should be formulated. A decrease in the number of people in poverty will result in less reliance by these individuals on government assistance programs for the basic necessities of life. A reduction in poverty levels, then, will lead to a decrease in hunger.

12. The government should act to reduce the number of hungry children. This can be done by insuring that government food assistance programs serve all eligible children.

13. Nutritional needs and access to food assistance programs for the homeless population should be addressed.

14. The reliance on more than one assistance program should be investigated. Benefit levels of these programs should be reviewed in order to determine if inadequate benefit levels are causing reliance on several programs. Furthermore, the government should investigate the consolidation of programs in order to minimize paperwork and bureaucracy.

15. Further investigation of meta-analysis as a tool for the study of survey research should be undertaken.

Appendix

Hunger Surveys

Clancy, K., et al. 1989. *Audit and evaluation of food program use in New York State: Report on phase one, Upstate food pantries.* New York: Author.   n=311

Clancy, K., et al. 1989. *Audit and evaluation of food program use in New York State: Report on phase one, New York City food pantries.* New York: Author.   n=208

Clancy, K., et al. 1989. *Audit and evaluation of food program use in New York State: Report on phase one, New York City soup kitchens.* New York: Author.   n=269

Community Action Committee of the Lehigh Valley, Inc. 1989. *The contradiction of lines among prosperity: A survey of the participants in the Lehigh Valley's emergency food assistance network.* Bethlehem, PA: Author.   n=190

Crossroads Urban Center and University of Utah Graduate School of Social Work. 1986. *We are the world, too!, Hunger in Salt Lake County.* Salt Lake City: Author.   n=189

Health and Welfare Council of Nassau County.
1984. *Hunger in Nassau County*. Nassau
County, NY: Author.   n= 200

Hunger Action Network of New York State.
1987. *Food with dignity: A study of people
using food pantries in New York state*. Albany,
NY: Author.   n=1970

Hunger Task Force of Milwaukee, Inc. 1987.
*Hunger in Milwaukee--the invisible epidemic,
a survey of emergency food pantry clients*.
Milwaukee, WI: Author.   n=457

Indiana State Board of Health. 1986. *Hunger
in Allen County*. Indianapolis, IN: Author.   n=218

Metro-Dade Community Action Agency. 1985.
Hunger in Dade County, Florida. Dade County,
FL: Author.   n=2134

Metropolitan Lutheran Ministry. 1985.
*Preliminary report: Hunger risk test and
nutrition/consumer informative survey*. Kansas
City, MO: Author.   n=418

Minnesota Food Education Resource Center. 1985.
Homegrown hunger. Minneapolis, MN: Author.   n=13,176

Montefiore Medical Center, Department of Social
Medicine. 1984. *Hunger watch — New York State,
Part I: Profile of "at-risk" populations and
service agencies*. New York: Author.   n=446

National Student Campaign Against Hunger.
1986. *Portrait of America's hungry*.
Washington, DC: Author.   n=1,574

National Student Campaign Against Hunger.
1987. *Portrait of America's Hungry: The
second annual survey of emergency food
recipients*. Washington, DC: Author.   n=1,876

Northern California Anti-Hunger Coalition, Data
Committee. 1984. *Hunger Survey, A survey
of recipients of emergency food assistance
in San Francisco, Alameda and Santa Cruz
counties*. Sacramento, CA: Author.   n=119

Ohio Senate Hunger Task Force. 1984. *Final
Report*. Columbus, OH: Author.   n=369

Oregon Food Share. 1986. *Profiles of the
hungry*. Portland OR: Author.   n=913

Rhode Island Emergency Food and Shelter Board
and United Way of Southeastern New England,
Inc. 1985. *Rhode Island's emergency food
and shelter needs*. Providence, RI: Author.   n=83

Spokane Food Bank, Inc. 1989. *Annual
client survey*. Spokane, WA: Author.   n=2,287

Summit County Hunger Study Task Force.
1988. *Study of hunger center users in Summit
County*. Akron, OH: Author.   n=369

Syracuse University, Department of Nutrition
and Food Management. 1989. *Audit and
evaluation of food program use in New York
State: In-depth economic study of clients in
Nassau County*. Syracuse: Author.   n=32

Syracuse University, Department of Nutrition
and Food Management. 1989. *Audit and
evaluation of food program use in New York
State: In-depth economic study of clients in
New York City*. Syracuse: Author.   n=103

Syracuse University, Department of Nutrition
and Food Management. 1989. *Audit and
evaluation of food program use in New York
State: In-depth economic study of clients in
upstate, rural setting*. Syracuse: Author.   n=66

Syracuse University, Department of Nutrition
and Food Management. 1989. *Audit and
evaluation of food program use in New York
State: In-depth economic study of clients in
upstate, urban setting*. Syracuse: Author.   n=101

Utahns Against Hunger and Utah Department of
Health, Division of Family Services. 1986.
*Utah nutrition monitoring project: Study of
low income households*. Salt Lake City: Author.   n=1,020

Wisconsin Nutrition Project. 1984. *Hunger
in Wisconsin*. Madison, WI: Author.   n=2,176

Bibliography

Avruch, S., and A.P. Cackley. 1995. Savings achieved by giving WIC benefits to women prenatally. *Public Health Reports* 110,1:27-34.

Backinger, C.L., S.B. Corbin, and L.J. Furman. 1988. Smokeless tobacco use in the United States: Health implications and policy options. *Journal of Public Health Policy* 9, 4:485-502.

Bailar, J.C. 1995. The practice of meta-analysis. *Journal of Clinical Epidemiology* 48, 1:149-157.

Bangert-Drowns, R.L. 1986. Review of developments in meta-analytic method. *Psychological Bulletin*, 99:388-399.

Barrett, D.E.,M. Radke-Yarrow, and R.E. Klein. 1982. Chronic malnutrition and child behavior: Effects of early caloric supplementation on social and emotional functioning at school age. *Developmental Psychology* 18, 4:541-556.

Bazzoli, G.J. 1985. Health care for the indigent: Overview of critical issues. *Health Services Research* 21, 3:353-393.

Berry, J.M. 1984. *Feeding Hungry People: Rulemaking in the Food Stamp Program*. New Brunswick, NJ: Rutgers University Press.

Bradford, W. 1953. *Of Plymouth Plantation 1620-1647*. New York: Alfred A. Knopf.

Brams, J.S., and D.L. Coury. 1985. Primary prevention of failure to thrive. In *New Directions in Failure to Thrive: Implications for Research and Practice*, ed. D.Drotar, 317-336. New York: Plenum Press.

Bremner, R.H. 1988. *American Philanthropy*. 2nd ed. Chicago: The University of Chicago Press.

Brown, G.E. 1984. National Nutrition Monitoring System: A Congressional perspective. *Journal of the American Dietetic Association* 84:1185-1189.

Brown, J.E. 1990. *The Science of Human Nutrition*. New York: Harcourt, Brace, Jovanovich.

Brown, J.L. 1987. Hunger in the U.S. *Scientific American* 256, 2:37-41.
—. 1989. When violence has a benevolent face: The paradox of hunger in the world's wealthiest democracy. *International Journal of Health Services* 19, 2:257-277.
Brown, J.L. and D. Allen. 1988. Hunger in America. *Annual Review of Public Health*, 9:503-526.
Brown, R.E. 1979. The young child: Failure to thrive. In *Nutrition and Growth*, eds. D.B. Jelliffe and E.F.P. Jelliffe. New York: Plenum Press.
Buescher,P.A., L.C. Larson, M.D. Nelson, Jr., and A.J. Lenihan. 1993. Prenatal WIC participation can reduce low birth weight and newborn medical costs: A cost-benefit analysis of WIC participation in North Carolina. *Journal of the American Dietetic Association* 93, 2:163-166.
Bullock, R.J., and D.J.Svyantek. 1985. Analyzing meta-analysis: Potential problems, an unsuccessful replication, and evaluation criteria. *Journal of Applied Psychology* 70, 1:108-115.
Chalmers, I. 1990. Underreporting research is scientific misconduct. *Journal of theAmerican Medical Association* 263:1405-1408.
Chandra, R.K. 1983. *Critical Reviews in Tropical Medicine.* New York: Macmillan.
—. 1991. 1990 McCollum Award Lecture. Nutrition and immunity: Lessons from the past and new insights into the future. *American Journal of Clinical Nutrition* 53:1087-1101.
Chwang, L., A.G. Soemantri, and E. Pollitt. 1988. Iron supplementation and physical growth of rural Indonesian children. *American Journal of Clinical Nutrition* 47:496-501.
Citizens' Board of Inquiry into Hunger and Malnutrition in the United States. 1968. *Hunger, U.S.A.: A report.* Boston: Beacon Press.
Congressional Budget Office. 1977. *The Food Stamp Program: Income or food supplementatiori?* Washington, D.C.: Congressional Budget Office.
Congressional Quarterly Almanac. 1984. Legislative Summary, Food Programs. *Congressional Quarterly Almanac*, 40:29.
—. 1983. Hunger Reports Prompt Food Aid Expansion. *Congressional Quarterly Almanac*, 39:412-416.
—. 1988. White House Announces Four 'Pocket Vetoes'. *Congressional Quarterly Almanac*, 44: 23-C.
Connecticut Association For Human Services 1986. Community Childhood Hunger Identification Project: Hunger Correlate Pilot Study. New Haven, CT: Connecticut Association For Human Services.

Cordray, D.S.1990. Strengthening causal interpretations of nonexperimental data: The role of meta-analysis. In *Research Methodology: Strengthening Causal Interpretations of Nonexperimental Data*, eds. L. Sechrest, E. Perris, and J. Bunker, 151-172. Washington, DC: U.S. Government Printing Office. DHHS publication [PHS] 90-3454.

Dallman, P.R., R. Yip, and C. Johnson. 1984. Prevalence and causes of anemia in the United States, 1976 to 1980. *American Journal of Clinical Nutrition* 39:437-445.

Dawson, E.B., and W.J. McGanity. 1987. Protection of maternal iron stores in pregnancy. *Journal of Reproductive Medicine* 32, (Suppl. 6): 478-487.

DeVault, M.L., and J.P. Pitts. 1984. Surplus and scarcity: Hunger and the origins of the Food Stamp Program. *Social Problems* 31, 5:545-557.

Dickersin, K. 1990. The existence of publication bias and risk factors for its occurrence. *Journal of the American Medical Association* 263:1385-1389.

Dickersin, K., and J.A. Berlin. 1992. Meta-analysis: State-of-the-science. *Epidemiologic Reviews*, 14:154-176.

Egan, M.C. 1994. Public health nutrition: A historical perspective. *Journal of the American Dietetic Association* 94, 3:298-304.

Emmons, L. 1986. Food procurement and the nutritional adequacy of diets in low-income families. *Journal of the American Dietetic Association* 86:1684-1693.

Fernandez, E., and D.C. Turk. 1989. The utility of cognitive coping strategies for altering pain perception: A meta-analysis. *Pain* 38, 2:123-135.

Fiske, D.W. 1983. The meta-analytic revolution in outcome research. *Journal of Consulting and Clinical Psychology* 51, 1:65-70.

Frank, D.A., D. Allen, and J.L. Brown. 1985. Primary prevention of failure to thrive: Social policy implications. In *New Directions in Failure to Thrive: Implications for Research and Practice*, ed. D. Drotar, 337-357. New York: Plenum Press.

Franz, M. 1981. Nutritional requirements of the elderly. *Journal of Nutrition for the Elderly* 1, 2:39-56.

Freeman, H.E., R.E. Klein, J. Kagan, and C. Yarbrough. 1977. Relations between nutrition and cognition in rural Guatemala. *American Journal of Public Health* 67, 3:233-239.

Galler, J.R., and F. Ramsey. 1989. A follow-up study of the influence of early malnutrition on development: Behavior at home and at school. *Journal of the American Academy of Child and Adolescent Psychiatry* 28, 2:254-261.

Glass, G.V. 1976. Primary, secondary, and meta-analysis research. *Educational Researcher*, 5:3-8.

Glass, G.V., and R.M. Kliegl. 1983. An apology for research integration in the study of psychotherapy. *Journal of Consulting and Clinical Psychology*, 51, 28-41.

Goodman, S.N. 1989. Meta-analysis and evidence. *Controlled Clinical Trials* 10, 2: 188-204.

Goodwin, J. S. 1989. Social, psychological and physical factors affecting the nutritional status of elderly subjects: Separating cause and effect. *American Journal of Clinical Nutrition* 50, (Suppl. 5):1201-1209.

Guthrie, H.A. 1979. *Introductory Nutrition.* 4th edition. St. Louis: The C.V. Mosby Company.

Haas, J.D., and M.W. Fairchild. 1989. Summary and conclusions of the International Conference on Iron Deficiency and Behavioral Development, October 10-12, 1988. *American Journal of Clinical Nutrition* 50, (Suppl. 3):703-705.

Hall, J.A., and M.C. Dornan. 1990. Patient sociodemographic characteristics as predictors of satisfaction with medical care: A meta-analysis. *Social Science and Medicine* 30, 7:811-818.

Hanft, R.S. 1981. Use of social science data for policy analysis and policy-making. *Health and Society* 59, 4:596-613.

Harris Survey, L. 1984. One in eleven American families suffering from hunger. New York: Tribune Company Syndicate.

Hasselblad, V., F. Mosteller, B. Littenberg, T.C. Chalmers, M.G.M. Hunink, J.A. Turner, S.C. Morton, P. Diehr, J.B. Wong, J and N.R. Powe. 1995. A survey of current problems in meta-analysis. *Medical Care* 33, 2:202-220.

Hediger, M.L., T.O. Scholl, D.H. Belsky, I.G. Ances, and R.W. Salmon. 1989. Patterns of weight gain in adolescent pregnancy: Effects on birth weight and preterm delivery. *Obstetrics and Gynecology* 74, 1:6-12.

Hultsman, J.T., and D.R. Black. 1989. Primary meta-analysis in leisure research: Results from Neulinger's "What am I doing?" instrument. *Journal of LeisureResearch*, 21:18-31.

Hunter, R. 1904. *Poverty.* New York: Macmillan.

Ibrahim, M.A. 1985. *Epidemiology and Health Policy.* Rockville, MD: Aspen.

Institute of Medicine 1985. *Preventing Low Birthweight.* Washington, DC: National Academy Press.

Jelliffe, D.B., and E.F.P. Jelliffe. 1989. *Community Nutritional Assessment.* New York: Oxford University Press.

Jenicek, M. 1989. Meta-analysis in medicine. *Journal of Clinical Epidemiology* 42,1:35-44.

Jones, D.R. 1995. Meta-analysis: Weighing the evidence. *Statistics in Medicine,* 14:137-149.

Kinsey, J.D. 1994. Food and Families' Socioeconomic Status. *Journal of Nutrition* 124, 9:1878s-1885s.

Kite, M.E., and B.T. Johnson. 1988. Attitudes toward older and younger adults: A meta-analysis. *Psychology and Aging* 3, 3:233-244.

Kleinman, J.C., and S.S. Kessel. 1987. Racial differences in low birth weight: Trends and risk factors. *The New England Journal of Medicine* 317, 12:749-753.

Kotelchuck, M., J.B. Schwartz, M.T. Anderka, and K.S. Finison. (1984). WIC participation and pregnancy outcomes: Massachusetts Statewide Evaluation Project. *American Journal of Public Health,* 74:10.

Kotz, N. 1969. *Let Them Eat Promises: The Politics of Hunger in America.* Englewood Cliffs, N.J.: Prentice-Hall, Inc.

Kramer, M.S., R.H. McLean, M. Olivier, D.M. Willis, and R.H. Usher. 1989. Body proportionality and head and length 'sparing' in growth-retarded neonates: A critical reappraisal. *Pediatrics* 84, 4:717-723.

Lechtig, A., H. Delgado, R. Martorell, C.Yarbrough, and R.E. Klein. 1979. Maternofetal nutrition. In *Nutrition and Growth,* eds. D.B. Jelliffe and E.F.P. Jelliffe. New York: Plenum Press.

Leinwand, G. 1985. *Hunger and malnutrition.* New York: Franklin Watts.

Liberati,A. 1995. "Meta-analysis:Statistical alchemy for the 21st century":Discussion. A plea for a more balanced view of meta-analysis and systematic overviews of the effect of health care interventions. *Journal of Clinical Epidemiology*48,1:81-86.

Light and Pillemer. 1984. *Summing up: The Science of Reviewing Research.* Cambridge, MA: Harvard University Press.

Life Sciences Research Office. 1985. Summary of a report on assessment of the iron nutritional status of the United States population. *American Journal of Clinical Nutrition,* 42:1318-1330.

Listernick, R., K. Christoffel, J. Pace, and J. Chiaramonte. 1985. Severe primary malnutrition in US children. *American Journal of Diseases of Children,* 139:1157-1160.

Louis, T.A., H.V. Fineberg, and F. Mosteller. 1985. Findings for public health from meta-analyses. *Annual Review of Public Health*, 6:1-20.

Marmor, T.R. 1970. *The Politics of Medicare.* New York: Aldine Publishing Company.

Massachusetts Department of Public Health 1983. *1983 Massachusetts Nutrition Survey.* Boston: Massachusetts Department of Public Health.

McCartney, K., M.J. Harris, and F. Bernieri. 1990. Growing up and growing apart: A developmental meta-analysis of twin studies. *Psychological Bulletin* 107, 2:226-237.

McCormick, M.C. 1985. The contribution of low birth weight to infant mortality and childhood morbidity. *The New England Journal of Medicine* 312, 2:82-90.

McGinnis, J.M., and M. Nestle. 1989. The Surgeon General's report on nutrition and health: Policy implications and implementation strategies. *American Journal of Clinical Nutrition*, 49:23-8.

McGovern, G.S. 1964. *War Against Want: America's Food for Peace Program.* New York: Walker.

Meinert, C.L. 1989. Meta-analysis: Science or religion? *Controlled Clinical Trials* 10, (4 suppl):257s-263s.

Minkler, M. 1984. Health promotion in long-term care: A contradiction in terms? *Health Education Quarterly* 11, 1:77-89.

Nagasawa, M., M.C. Smith, J.H. Barnes, and J.E. Fincham. 1990. Meta-analysis of correlates of diabetes patients' compliance with prescribed medications. *The Diabetes Educator* 16, 3:192-200.

National Academy of Sciences 1990. *Nutrition During Pregnancy.* Washington, DC: National Academy Press.

Nestle, M., and S. Guttmacher. 1989, October. *Hunger in the United States: Rationale, Methods, and Policy Implications of State Hunger Surveys.* Paper presented at the annual meeting of the American Public Health Association, Chicago.

Neustadt, R.E., and H.V. Fineberg. 1978. *The Swine Flu Affair: Decision-Making on a Slippery Disease.* Washington, DC: Department of Health, Education, and Welfare.

O'Rourke, K., and A.S. Detsky. 1989. Meta-analysis in medical research: Strong encouragement for higher quality in individual research efforts. *Journal of Clinical Epidemiology* 42, 10:1021-1024.

Oski, F.A., A.S. Honig, B. Helu, and P. Howanitz. 1982. Effect of iron therapy on behavior performance in nonanemic, iron deficient infants. *Pediatrics* 71, 6:877- 880.

Patterson, B.H., and G. Block. 1988. Food choices and the cancer guidelines. *American Journal of Public Health* 78, 3:282-286.

Physician Task Force on Hunger in America. (1985). *Hunger in America: The Growing Epidemic.* Middletown, CT: Wesleyan University Press.

—. (1986). Hunger Counties 1986: *The Distribution of America's High-Risk Areas.* Cambridge, MA: Harvard University, School of Public Health.

Polhamus, B., K.E.Peterson, and P.Miller. 1989, October. *Psychological and Biological Risk Factors Associated With Failure-to-Thrive in Children Referred for Multidisciplinary Treatment.* Paper presented at the annual meeting of the American Public Health Association, Chicago.

Pollitt, E. 1994. Poverty and child development: Relevance of research in developing countries to the United States. *Child Development,*65:283-295.

Pollitt, E., and Leibel, R.L. 1976. Iron deficiency and behavior. *Journal of Pediatrics*, 88, 372-381.

Pollitt,E., R.L. Leibel, and D. Greenfield. 1991. Brief fasting, stress and cognition in children. *American Journal of Clinical Nutrition*, 34:1526-1533.

Posner, B.M., A. Jette, C. Smigelski, D. Miller, and P. Mitchell. 1994. Nutritional risk in New England elders. *Journal of Gerontology* 49, 3:M123-M132.

Posner, B.M., A.M. Jette, K.W. Smith, and D.R. Miller. 1993. Nutrition and health risks in the elderly: The nutrition screening initiative. *American Journal of Public Health* 83:972-978.

Powe,N.R., J.A.Turner, C.W. Maklan, and M. Ersek. 1994. Alternative methods for formal literature review and meta-analysis in AHCPR patient outcomes research teams. *Medical Care* 32,7:JS22-JS37, supplement.

President's Task Force on Food Assistance. 1984. *Report of the President's Task Force on Food Assistance.* Washington, DC: 726 Jackson Place, N.W.

Robinson, C.H., M.R. Lawler, W.L. Chenoweth, and A.E. Garwick. 1986. *Normal and Therapeutic Nutrition.* 17th ed. New York: Macmillan.

Rolfes, S.R., L.K. DeBruyne, and E.N. Whitney. 1990. *Life span nutrition: Conception Through Life.* New York: West Publishing Company.

Rothstein, H.R., and M.A. McDaniel. 1989. Guidelines for conducting and reporting meta-analyses. *Psychological Reports*, 65:759-770.

Rush, D., Sloan, N.L., Leighton, J., Alvir, J.M., Horvitz, D.G., Seaver, W.B., Garbowski, G.C., Johnson, S.S., Kulka, R.A., Holt, M., Devore, J.W., Lynch, J.T., Woodside, M.B., and Shanklin, D.S. 1988. Longitudinal study of pregnant women. *American Journal of Clinical Nutrition* 48, (Suppl. 2): 439-483.

Saloutos, T. 1982. *The American Farmer and the New Deal*. Ames, IA: The Iowa State University Press.

Schapsmeier, E.L., and F.H. Schapsmeier. 1975. *Encyclopedia of American Agricultural History*. Westport, CT: Greenwood Press.

Shannon, B.M., H. Smiciklas-Wright, B.W. Davis, and C. Lewis. 1983. A peer educator approach to nutrition for the elderly. *Gerontologist* 23, 2:123-126.

Shapiro, S., M.C. McCormick, B.H. Starfield, J.P. Krischer, and D. Bross. 1980. Relevance of correlates of infant deaths for significant morbidity at 1 year of age. *American Journal of Obstetrics and Gynecology* 136, 3:363-373.

Singh, G.K., and Yu, S.M. 1995. Infant mortality in the United States: Trends, differentials, and projections, 1950 through 2010. *American Journal of Public Health*, 85:957-964.

Slavin, R.E. 1995. Best evidence synthesis: An intelligent alternative to meta-analysis. *Journal of Clinical Epidemiology* 48, 1:9-18.

Solomon, M.A., and S.M. Shortell. 1981. Designing health policy research for utilization. *Health Policy Quarterly* 1, 3:216-237.

Stockbauer, J.W. 1986. Evaluation of the Missouri WIC program: Prenatal components. *Journal of the American Dietetic Association* 86, 1: 61-67.

Strube, M.J., and D.P. Hartmann. 1982. A critical appraisal of meta-analysis. *British Journal of Psychology*, 21:129-139.

Strube, M.J., and D.P. Hartmann. 1983. Meta-analysis techniques, applications, and functions. *Journal of Consulting and Clinical Psychology* 51, 1:14-27.

Taffel, S.M., and K.G. Keppel. 1986. Advice about weight gain during pregnancy and actual weight gain. *American Journal of Public Health* 76, 12:1396-1399.

Terris, M. 1986. Epidemiology and the public health movement. *Journal of Chronic Diseases* 39, 12:953-961.

U.S. Conference of Mayors 1982. *Human Services in FY82: Shrinking Resources in Troubled Times, A Survey of Human Services Officials in the Nation's Cities*. Washington, DC: U.S. Conference of Mayors.

—. 1983a. *Hunger in American Cities, Eight Case Studies*. Washington, DC: U.S. Conference of Mayors.

—. 1983b. *Responses to Urban Hunger, Public-Private Efforts to Provide Emergency Food Assistance in America's Cities.* Washington, DC: U.S. Conference of Mayors.

—. 1984. *Task Force on Joblessness and Hunger Status Report: Emergency Food, Shelter, and Energy Programs in 20 Cities.* Washington, DC: U.S. Conference of Mayors.

—. 1986a. *The Growth of Hunger, Homelessness and Poverty in America's Cities in 1985, A 25-City Survey.* Washington, DC: U.S. Conference of Mayors.

—. 1986b. *The Continued Growth of Hunger, Homelessness and Poverty In America's Cities: 1986, A 25-City Survey.* Washington, DC: U.S. Conference of Mayors.

—. 1987a. *A Status Report on Homeless Families in America's Cities, A 29-City Survey.* Washington, DC: U.S. Conference of Mayors.

—. 1987b. *The Continuing Growth of Hunger, Homelessness and Poverty in America's Cities: 1987, A 26-City Survey.* Washington, DC: U.S. Conference of Mayors.

—. 1988. *Barriers to Participation in Benefit Programs, A 38-City Survey.* Washington, DC: U.S. Conference of Mayors.

—. 1989. *A Status Report on Hunger and Homelessness in America's Cities: 1989, A 27-city Survey.* Washington, DC: U.S. Conference of Mayors.

U.S. Congress 1946. *National School Lunch Act*, Public Law 396.

—. 1964. *Food Stamp Act of 1964*, Public Law 88-525, 7 U.S.C. §§ 2030-2032.

—. 1965. *Older Americans Act of 1965*, Public Law 89-73, 42 U.S.C. §§ 3001,3002,3011,3012,3021-3025,3031,3032,3041,3042,3051-3053.

—. 1966. *Child Nutrition Act of 1966*, Public Law 89-642, 42 U.S.C. §§ 1771-1789.

—. U.S. Congress 1971. *Food Stamp Act of 1964*, amendments, Public Law 91-671, 7 U.S.C. §§ 2048-2052.

—. U.S. Congress 1972. *Older Americans Act of 1965*, amendment, Public Law 92-258, 42 U.S.C. §§ 3045-3045i, 3051-3055.

—. U.S. Congress 1972. *National School Lunch Act*, amendment, Public Law 92-433, 42 U.S.C. §§ 1756-1759,1761.

—. U.S. Congress 1977. *Food and Agriculture Act of 1977*, Public Law 95-113, 7 U.S.C. §§ scattered.

—. U.S. Congress 1981. *Agriculture and Food Act of 1981*, Public Law 97-98, 7 U.S.C. §§ scattered (repealed).

—. U.S. Congress 1987. *Stewart B. McKinney Homeless Assistance Act,* Public Law 100-77, 42 U.S.C. §§ scattered.

—. U.S. Congress 1989. *Child Nutrition and WIC Reauthorization Act of 1989,* Public Law 101-147, 42 U.S.C. §§ scattered.

—. U.S. Congress 1990. *National Nutrition Monitoring and Related Research Act of 1990,* Public Law 101-445, 7 U.S.C. §§ 5301,5302,5311-5316,5331,5332,5341,5342.

U.S. Department of Health and Human Services, Public Health Service. 1979. *Healthy People: The Surgeon General's Report on Disease Prevention and Health Promotion* (DHHS Publication No. PHS 79-5507). Washington, DC: U.S. Government Printing Office.

—. U.S. Department of Health and Human Services. 1988. *The Surgeon General's Report on Nutrition and Health.* (DHHS Publication No. PHS 88-50210). Washington, DC: U.S. Government Printing Office.

—. U.S. Department of Health and Human Services. 1989. *Nutrition Monitoring in the United States: An Update Report on Nutrition Monitoring.* (DHHS Publication No. PHS 89-1255). Washington, DC: U.S. Government Printing Office.

—. U.S. Department of Health and Human Services. 1991. *Healthy People 2000: National Health Promotion and Disease Prevention Objectives.* (DHHS Publication No. PHS 91-50212). Washington, DC: U.S. Government Printing Office.

—. U.S. Department of Health and Human Services. 1995. *Health United States 1994.* (DHHS Publication No. PHS 95-1232). Washington, DC: U.S. Government Printing Office.

U.S. Department of Health and Human Services and U.S. Department of Agriculture. 1986. *Nutrition Monitoring in the United States–A Progress Report from the Joint Nutrition Monitoring Evaluation Committee.* (DHHS Publication No. PHS 86-1255). Washington, DC: U.S. Government Printing Office.

U.S. General Accounting Office. 1983. *Public and Private Efforts to Feed America's Poor.* (GAO Publication No. RCED-83-164). Washington, DC: U.S. General Accounting Office.

—. U.S. General Accounting Office. 1986. *Hunger Counties: Methodological Review of a Report by the Physician Task Force on Hunger.* (GAO Publication No. PEMD-86-7BR). Washington, DC: U.S. General Accounting Office.

U.S. House of Representatives. 1976. *Food Stamp Act of 1976.* (Report No. 94-1460). Washington, DC: 94th U.S. Congress.

—. U.S. House of Representatives. 1985a. *A Review of the Thrifty Food Plan, and its Use in the Food Stamp Program*. Washington, DC: U.S. House of Representatives, Subcommittee on Domestic Marketing, Consumer Relations, and Nutrition of the Committee on Agriculture.

—. U.S. House of Representatives. 1985b. *The Food Stamp Program*. Washington, DC: U.S. House of Representatives, Committee on Agriculture, Nutrition, and Forestry.

U.S. Senate. 1977. *Federally Supported Food Programs*. Washington, DC: U.S. Senate, Select Committee on Nutrition and Human Needs.

Waterlow, J.C. 1972. Classification and definition of protein-calorie malnutrition. *The British Medical Journal*, 3:566-569.

Wegman, M.E. 1985. Annual summary of vital statistics. *Pediatrics*, 74: 981-990.

Weimer, J.P. 1983. The nutritional status of the elderly. *Journal of Nutrition for the Elderly* 2, 3:17-25.

Winick, M. (Ed.). 1979. *Hunger disease: Studies by the Jewish Physicians in the Warsaw Ghetto*. New York: John Wiley & Sons.

Wisconsin Nutrition Project 1984. *Hunger in Wisconsin*. Madison, WI: Wisconsin Nutrition Project.

Wolf, F.M. 1986. *Meta-analysis: Quantitative Methods for Research Synthesis*. Beverly Hills, CA: Sage Publications.

Wolinsky, F.D., J.M. Prendergast, D.K. Miller, R.M. Coe, and M.N. Chavez. 1985. A preliminary validation of a nutritional risk measure for the elderly. *American Journal of Preventive Medicine* 1, 2:53-59.

Wortman, P.M. 1983. Meta-analysis: A validity perspective. *Annual Review of* Psychology, 34:223-260.

Index

Printed in the United States
by Baker & Taylor Publisher Services